SKEWER COOKING
ON THE GRILL

Bob and Coleen Simmons

BRISTOL PUBLISHING ENTERPRISES
San Leandro, California

A Nitty Gritty® Cookbook

©1995, Bristol Publishing Enterprises, Inc.,
P.O. Box 1737, San Leandro, California 94577.

Printed in the United States of America.

ISBN 1-55867-122-6

Cover design: Frank Paredes
Cover photography: John Benson
Food stylist: Suzanne Carreiro
Illustrator: James Balkovek

CONTENTS

SKEWER COOKING

Call them kabobs, shish kabobs, shashlik, souvlakia, spiedini or brochettes, and you conjure up artful images of succulent, beautifully grilled pieces of meat and vegetables on a skewer. Early man probably used twigs to support pieces of meat over fire, and modern man has continued to refine this cooking technique. Kabobs are thought to have originated in the Middle East, with chunks of meat cooked on soldiers' swords, and the cuisines of this region still feature a great variety of foods cooked on skewers. Asian countries too, use skewers for satays, yakitori and hibachi cooking. Skewer cooking is a natural for the grill wherever you are in the world.

Kabob cooking is fun! Kabobs are festive! Kabobs are colorful and delicious! Recipes are simple and easily prepared ahead of time. Cooking time is short. Kabobs work well for family and special meals, snacks, appetizers, entrées or desserts. Kabobs can be tailored easily to accommodate personal food preferences. Have a skewer party with participants assembling and grilling their own special combinations.

Part of the enjoyment of skewer cooking is pairing savory grilled foods with a delicious side dish or salad. Included are some favorite rice dishes, an easy microwaved polenta, bean and vegetable salads, and salsas.

Get out the grill and try some of these easy, delicious kabob recipes!

GRILLING TIPS

- To get great food from the grill, start with the freshest, highest quality ingredients.
- Rinse chicken or fish under cold running water and pat dry before placing in marinade. Be sure to wash hands, knives and cutting boards with hot soapy water after handling poultry and fish.
- Meats cooked on skewers do not get more tender as they grill; therefore, it is essential to use lean cuts, trimmed of all fat and connective tissue. The best cuts are from the tenderloin, loin and leg. Fish should be very fresh and cooked only until the flesh "sets," not until dry.
- Do not marinate chicken or fish longer than 20 minutes at room temperature. Cover with marinade and refrigerate; then bring out 10 to 15 minutes before grilling. When marinating at room temperature, choose a cool place, out of the sun.
- Always have a clean plate ready to receive cooked foods from the grill. Do not put cooked foods back on plates or boards used for cutting up raw ingredients.
- Preheat your grill for at least 10 minutes before starting to grill. If using charcoal, you will want a nice bed of evenly glowing coals for cooking.
- Approximate cooking times are given as guidelines for grilling in this book. Each type of grill cooks differently. It may take slightly longer to cook meats on a gas grill than on a hot charcoal fire, but if the charcoal fire has substantially burned down, or if the

cooking racks are too high over the fire, foods will take longer to grill.

- Get a good "instant read" meat thermometer to check for doneness. Learn to test for doneness by poking the food with a finger. As meat and fish cook, they tend to firm up; with practice you can learn to tell when food is cooked to the proper doneness. Thin slices of meat or ground meat will start to show droplets of moisture on the uncooked surface about the time they are half cooked, which indicates they are ready to be turned. Meat usually is cooked for slightly less time on the second side; a general guideline is 60 percent on the first side, and 40 percent on the second.

- Presoak wood skewers for 20 to 30 minutes before using to avoid burning the ends.

- Brush food lightly with olive oil or butter, or spray with nonstick cooking spray, before placing on the grill, particularly if it hasn't been marinated. It is helpful to oil cooking racks before grilling fish and chicken.

- If you plan to serve both meat and cooked vegetables on skewers, put the meat on one skewer and the vegetables on another, unless they have similar cooking times. Thin squares of onions or peppers generally will cook in the same amount of time as meat, and make an attractive presentation when alternated with the meat. Chunks of carrots or potatoes, unless partially precooked, will not cook as fast as the meat.

- The grill should be cleaned after each use. This is particularly important with seafood. A preheating grill that smells of the last food that was cooked on it probably wasn't properly cleaned and may lend some "off" flavors to the food to be cooked.

EQUIPMENT

GRILLS

Skewered foods may be cooked over a variety of heat sources.

Charcoal grill - This is the oldest and still the best heat source for cooking skewered food. As juices vaporize on the coals, they flavor the food. No other heat source does this. The best charcoal grills allow you to control the distance of the food from the coals. Different foods need to be cooked at different heat intensities. Meat that is to be eaten rare needs a very hot fire. Vegetables that take longer to cook need to be farther from the fire so that they don't burn on the outside before they cook through.

Gas grill - A good gas grill is almost as effective as a charcoal grill in producing favorable, juicy skewers. Most gas grills have a heat control which allows greater control over the cooking process. Grills should always be preheated according to manufacturer's directions.

Indoor stovetop grill - Built-in grills, such as the Jenn Air, supply more heat than tabletop grills, and can do a very nice job of cooking food on skewers. When the weather outside is particularly cold or rainy, an indoor grill provides an attractive alternative to a charcoal grill.

Electric tabletop grill - Electric tabletop grills work particularly well with appetizer skewers. These are usually smaller than entrée skewers, and tend to be thinner, therefore needing less heat. Many tabletop grills don't have enough surface area to cook entrée skewers for more that two or three persons. Lower wattage units don't provide enough heat to properly sear the outside of the food and therefore it sometimes comes out dry and uninteresting.

Oven broiler - The broiler in a gas or electric oven can be used to cook skewers, if they can be placed close enough to the heat source. Place the skewers on a rack set into a broiler pan. Be sure to preheat the oven and broiler pan for several minutes before you start to cook.

Hibachi - A hibachi is effective in grilling small quantities of appetizer skewers. If you use the hibachi indoors, get it started outside and bring it inside only when the coals have burned down. If you have a hood over your stovetop, set the hibachi on a heavy cookie sheet on the burners so that cooking fumes and carbon monoxide can be safely exhausted. Some people put their hibachi in the fireplace to get rid of fumes and carbon monoxide. As soon as you are finished cooking, take the hibachi outside.

OTHER TOOLS

Here are some items that definitely assist the cook in grilling.

It is important to protect your hands and arms with **hot pan holders** or **mitts** while grilling. Metal skewer handles tend to get very hot during the grilling process.

Long-handled spring-loaded **tongs** work well to turn foods and keep you a comfortable distance from the fire. It is easy to grab the pointed end of longer skewers with tongs to help while you turn the cooler, or handle, end with your hand. Short skewers can often be turned with tongs alone. Tongs can also be used to prop the grill lid open an inch during cooking, to allow the skewer handles to protrude beyond the grilling area.

It is useful to have a **basting brush** with a long handle to help you keep your distance from the heat and to control the amount of marinade brushed on during the cooking process. Always wash the brush with hot soapy water after each use.

A **spatula** with a long handle and thin edge is very useful to loosen food stuck to the grill and to help turn more fragile foods.

We keep **service plates**, such as pie plates, cookie sheets and other stainless plates, on hand for assembling the ingredients, tossing the food with oil and lemon or other marinades, threading the food on skewers, and catching the marinade drips. It is also very important to transfer the cooked food to a clean plate and not reuse the plate on which the raw food was transported.

There are many different kinds of **skewers** available. **Bamboo skewers** come in many different lengths, and the most practical are at least 10 inches long. These must be soaked in water for 20 to 30 minutes before threading with food, or they have a tendency to burn. Exposed skewer ends may be wrapped in aluminum foil after skewers are assembled. Remove foil before serving. **Metal skewers** come in all sizes and lengths. Unless you are doing individual appetizer portions, a 12-inch length or longer is the most practical. Our favorite is an 18-inch-long flat-bladed stainless steel skewer. The blade is about $\frac{1}{8}$-inch wide and prevents skewered food from turning on the blade. Metal skewers can be washed in the dishwasher. Some skewers have $\frac{1}{8}$-inch square blades, and these work very well with vegetables. There are double metal skewers with flat blades that are useful for holding items that have a tendency to roll on a single skewer.

THE GRILLING PANTRY

Here are the some pantry items that make spur-of-the-moment skewer cooking an adventure.

Vinegar - The vinegar in a marinade not only livens up the flavor of grilled meat or fish, but it also helps to break down the fibers and tenderize the food. Vinegars are made by fermenting the sugars available in many fruit and vegetable products. Each has distinct flavor characteristics, and it is useful to have red wine, apple cider, rice wine (unsweetened), sherry wine and balsamic vinegars on hand. The rice wine and balsamic vinegars are generally less sharp. There are also intriguing herb- and fruit-flavored vinegars available. Vinegars keep indefinitely, so you can afford to keep an interesting variety in your pantry.

Oil - This is a vast subject. Most marinades need a little oil to keep foods from sticking to the grill. Oils add flavor as well.

One of the most helpful products for grilling is nonstick cooking spray. Use it to spray your cooking racks before putting them over the fire, for easier cleanup. It also works to spray a light coating over food to be grilled instead of brushing it with oil. There are several different kinds available, including an olive oil spray.

Olive oils are healthful as well as flavorful, and you will want to keep at least two different ones in your pantry: a light all-purpose oil for marinating delicate seafood dishes, and a fruity full-flavored oil for meat, poultry, vegetables and salad dressings. We like the heavier full-flavored extra virgin oil paired with herbs to give grilled foods a little extra complexity. It is wonderful brushed on Italian-style bread before toasting it. Olive oils lose their fruitiness with age, so buy the most recently harvested and pressed oils, in the quantity that you can use in a few weeks. Olive oil should be treated with care. Keep it tightly capped in a cool dark spot in your pantry.

Mustard - "Ball park" mustard is great for hamburgers and hot dogs, but when you grill, you need a mustard with more character. Mustard can add a subtle nuance or be a major ingredient in marinades. Keep a Dijon, a stone-ground, and a hot, sweet mustard on hand. A distinctively flavored mustard is one of the quickest flavor enhancers for grilling. Large shrimp or chicken breasts are delicious when grilled with nothing more than a generous coating of flavorful mustard and a little oil.

Prepared barbecue sauces - There are hundreds of barbecue sauces on the market, and finding a favorite can be a long and pleasant task. Since most barbecue sauces contain sugar and burn easily, they are usually brushed on during the last few minutes before serving.

Chicken stock - The very best chicken stock is one you make yourself, because you can control the salt and the quality. The fat-free and low sodium products available make acceptable substitutes.

Soy sauce - There are several different Chinese and Japanese soy sauces available that add a wonderful flavor to marinades when used in small quantities. There are some low sodium soy sauces available on the market.

Other Asian sauces

oyster sauce: This is made from oysters, but it does not have a strong fishy taste. It is particularly good in meat and chicken marinades.

hoisin sauce: This favorite marinade ingredient tastes both sweet and pungent and rounds out a strongly flavored marinade. It is made from soybeans, vinegar, chile peppers and spices.

Shaoxing rice wine: This is a lightly flavored, slightly sweet wine that is particularly good in fish and chicken marinades. Dry sherry is a good substitute.

Ginger - Always keep some fresh ginger root on hand. Buy firm, heavy pieces that do not look shriveled, and store them in the refrigerator in a plastic bag with a couple of holes for a little air circulation. Cut off a slice and peel before using. Small, flat Asian graters with rows of little sharp teeth work well for finely grating ginger.

Hot sauces and red pepper flakes - A dash or two of Tabasco, Crystal Hot Sauce, or your favorite green chile sauce brightenes most sauces, marinades and dips. The new green Jalapeño Sauce under the Tabasco brand is a very good product with a lively chile flavor and mild bite. Red pepper flakes add a nice zip to any marinade, as does a pinch of cayenne pepper.

Sun-dried tomatoes - These are available both dried and packed in olive oil. The dried tomato pieces should be reconstituted by steaming for 5 minutes, or softening in hot water. You can then add your own olive oil and some herbs and keep them in the refrigerator. The oil-packed tomatoes have already been softened and can be used as they come out of the jar. They are great used on kabobs to separate pieces of grilled meat, chicken or mushrooms.

The tomato-flavored olive oil that they are packed in makes a particularly delicious addition to salad dressings or marinades.

Chipotle chile peppers - This smoky, spicy pepper is available in small cans, usually packed in adobo sauce. It is extremely hot, and a small amount of the pepper and the vinegar-flavored sauce will produce a lot of punch.

Peppers - Fresh red, yellow or green sweet bell peppers, or hot varieties such as green chile, jalapeño, serrano and tiny Thai peppers, all add lots of color and flavor. Bell peppers can be grilled with or without peeling, or grilled whole until the skins are blackened, and then peeled and used in sauces or as dish accents. Jalapeño, serrano and Thai peppers generally are used sparingly to add flavor and character to marinades and salsas.

Beans - There are many good canned beans on the market, including black beans, garbanzo beans, small white beans, red beans and pinto beans. We use them in the interest of saving time, but you certainly could soak and cook beans from scratch if you like. We drain the canned beans, rinse them well with cold water, and then thoroughly drain them again before using them.

APPETIZER SKEWERS

A cookout is synonymous with having a party. Serve some nibbles before the main event or while waiting for the fire in the grill to get to the proper intensity.

Appetizers on skewers lend a festive air. Included are some traditional favorites with grilled wrapped figs, dates, mushrooms or artichokes. A hot pepper cheese fondue or spicy *Romesco Dip* with grilled seafood make great starters. During the summer, fresh fruit or vegetable chunks lightly grilled are light and delicious.

Double metal skewers or two parallel presoaked wood skewers work best for most of these grilled appetizers. Small pieces of vegetables or meat tend to roll when they are turned, and the double skewer holds them flat for easier turning and more even cooking.

Here are some easy and delicious ideas to get the party rolling.

GRILLED MARINATED MUSHROOMS

Makes: 20

Marinate the mushrooms a day ahead and then grill them for a quick appetizer. These are a terrific selection for an antipasto platter, grilled or not, or use them as a garnish for a salad or grilled meat.

1/4 cup full-flavored olive oil
1 large clove garlic, peeled, smashed
1/4 cup rice wine vinegar
dash red pepper flakes
1/4 tsp. sugar

1/2 tsp. dried thyme
1/2 tsp. dried basil
salt and freshly ground pepper
10 medium mushrooms, cleaned,
  stems removed, cut in half

Combine all ingredients, except mushrooms, in a small stainless steel saucepan. Bring to a boil, lower heat and simmer uncovered for 5 minutes. Add mushroom halves and simmer for an additional 5 minutes. Remove from heat and allow mushrooms to cool in liquid. These can be made ahead and refrigerated for 3 to 4 days. Remove from marinade and arrange on metal or presoaked wood skewers. Grill over medium heat for 3 to 4 minutes a side, turning once.

MUSHROOM AND PEPPER SKEWERS

Peppers and mushrooms are a delicious match. Thread them on rosemary skewers (see page 38), if you can get them, for extra flavor.

1 large red or green bell pepper, or ½ each color
10 marinated mushrooms with marinade, page 13
6 green onions, trimmed, cut into 1½-inch lengths

Remove pepper core and seeds; cut into 1- or 1½-inch squares. Alternate marinated mushrooms, pepper pieces and onions on metal or presoaked wood skewers. Brush peppers and onions with a little mushroom marinade. Grill over medium heat for 3 to 4 minutes a side, turning once. Brush with a little more marinade during grilling.

GRILLED MARINATED MUSHROOMS AND SHRIMP

Marinate fresh uncooked shrimp with the mushrooms for a few minutes. Fresh red pepper squares can be substituted for the tomato pieces.

10-15 medium-sized fresh shrimp,
  peeled, deveined
10 marinated mushrooms, cut in half,
  with marinade, page 13
2 plum tomatoes

Add shrimp to cooled mushroom marinade with mushrooms and let stand for 15 to 20 minutes. Remove tomato cores, cut tomatoes in half lengthwise and scoop out seeds. Cut each tomato half into 3 pieces. Alternate shrimp, mushroom halves and tomatoes on metal or presoaked wood skewers. Brush tomatoes with marinade. Grill over medium heat for 3 to 4 minutes a side, turning once, until shrimp are pink and slightly firm to the touch. Brush with marinade while cooking.

FIGS WRAPPED IN PROSCIUTTO

Makes: 20-24

When fresh figs are in season, buy the biggest, ripest ones you can find. Fresh ripe Comice or Bartlett pears, pieces of melon or peaches are delicious done this way, too.

10-12 fresh figs
lime or lemon juice
freshly ground pepper
6-8 fresh mint leaves, cut into fine strips
12-14 thin slices prosciutto

Cut off stem of each fig and a small slice from the bottom; cut into halves or quarters, depending on size of figs. Sprinkle cut sides of figs with a few drops of lime or lemon juice and a generous grind of pepper. Sprinkle with mint leaves. Cut prosciutto slices in half lengthwise and in pieces long enough to easily wrap around a fig. Place wrapped figs on metal or presoaked wood skewers and cook on a preheated grill for about 1 to 2 minutes a side, turning once, to lightly color prosciutto and to warm figs. Serve immediately.

HOT PEPPER CHEESE FONDUE
FOR SKEWERED VEGETABLES

If you don't have a fondue pot, use a heavy ceramic serving dish to hold this zesty dunking sauce. Grilled skewered crisp-tender vegetables make great dippers, but you can also use grilled whole wheat toast fingers or tortilla chips.

2 tbs. butter
2 tbs. flour
1½ cups milk
¼ tsp. dry mustard

6 oz. hot pepper Jack cheese, coarsely
  grated
2 tbs. grated Parmesan cheese

Stovetop: Melt butter in a small saucepan or fondue pot, add flour and cook for 2 minutes. Slowly stir in milk and cook until mixture thickens. Add dry mustard and both cheeses. Cook until cheese melts and mixture is hot.

Microwave: Use 1¼ cups milk and heat uncovered on high until milk is steaming. Combine flour with grated cheeses and stir into hot milk mixture. Stir in butter and mustard. Cook on medium for 2 minutes, stir, and continue to cook for another 1 to 2 minutes until cheeses are melted. Pour into a fondue pot or serving dish.

TOMATOES STUFFED WITH
GOAT CHEESE AND BLACK OLIVE PASTE

*Tomato halves are filled with a little goat cheese and black olive paste and heated on the grill until warm. They're good alone, or served as part of an antipasto plate with a little prosciutto or thin ham rolls, **Grilled Marinated Mushrooms**, page 13, and some crisp carrot or fennel sticks. Most supermarkets carry small jars of olive paste, sometimes called Olivado or tapenade, in the specialty foods section. These can be assembled a couple of hours ahead and left at room temperature until grilled.*

For each serving:
1 small ripe plum tomato
1 tsp. goat cheese
½ tsp. black olive paste

Cut tomatoes in half lengthwise; scoop out seeds and pulp. Lightly salt inside of shells and turn upside down to drain for 15 to 20 minutes. For each serving, spoon goat cheese into tomato shell and top with olive paste. Skewer tomato halves with metal or presoaked wood skewers through the middle of each, 2 or 3 per skewer. Skewers will help keep tomatoes upright and easier to handle while grilling. Place bottom side down on a preheated grill and cook for 4 to 5 minutes until tomato halves are warmed.

DATES WRAPPED IN PANCETTA

Delicious sweet Medjool or Dromedary dried dates are terrific wrapped in pancetta and grilled. If you don't have pancetta, use very thinly sliced bacon and blanch it or partially cook it for a minute or two in the microwave before wrapping dates.

8 dates
4 small green onions, white part only
4-8 slices pancetta or half-slices bacon

Remove pits from dates. Quarter green onions, cutting them vertically, so you have thin onion slivers. Push onions into slits left by date pits. Wrap each date with a piece of pancetta, or a half-slice of bacon, and arrange on metal or presoaked wood skewers. Grill over medium heat for 2 or 3 minutes a side until pancetta is crisp and brown.

GRILLED LEEK-WRAPPED SHRIMP KABOBS

Makes: 20-25

*Strips of leek make an attractive wrapper for shrimp or scallops. These can be made ahead of time and refrigerated until time to grill. Serve as they are, hot off the grill, or with **Romesco Dip**, page 21, or **European-Style Cocktail Sauce**, page 68.*

2 large leeks
1 tbs. olive oil
1 tbs. lemon juice
salt and freshly ground pepper
1 lb. large shrimp (20-25 per lb.), peeled, deveined

Trim away green part of leeks and cut off the root end. Cut white part of leeks in half lengthwise and wash out any sand. Boil some water in a large saucepan and blanch leeks for 2 to 3 minutes. Remove from pan, rinse with cold water and pat dry with paper towels. Cut into strips 1 inch wide x 3 inches long. Combine olive oil, lemon juice, salt and pepper. Toss shrimp in olive oil mixture, and then coat blanched leek strips in oil. Wrap a leek strip around each shrimp and thread on a metal or presoaked wood skewer. Cook on a preheated grill for about 3 to 4 minutes a side, or until shrimp are pink and leeks are lightly browned. Serve hot.

ROMESCO DIP

This is a terrific Spanish-style sauce to keep on hand for an appetizer dip. It keeps in the refrigerator for a few days and is perfect for dunking hot grilled shrimp or scallops, or serving with a platter of crisp carrot sticks, blanched green beans and other vegetables. Slather it over hot new potatoes or use it as a dip for crisp oven-roasted potato sticks. Stir in a little water if the sauce gets too thick. It should be the consistency of light cream.

2 tbs. full-flavored olive oil
1 slice white bread
1 cup peeled, seeded, chopped
  tomatoes
2 cloves garlic, minced
1/4 cup chopped onion
1/8 tsp. red pepper flakes

1 large red bell pepper, roasted,
  seeded, peeled
1/2 cup toasted almonds or hazelnuts
2 tbs. red wine vinegar
1/2 tsp. paprika
1/3 cup full-flavored olive oil
salt and freshly ground pepper

Heat 1 tbs. olive oil in a medium skillet and sauté bread on both sides until nicely browned. Set aside. Add 1 tbs. oil to skillet and sauté tomatoes, garlic, onion and red pepper flakes over medium heat for 4 to 5 minutes. Pour tomato mixture into a food processor bowl with remaining ingredients and bread. Process until quite smooth. Refrigerate until 30 minutes before serving.

GRILLED HAM-WRAPPED SCALLOPS

Servings: 4-6

Cut Danish ham slices into strips the same width as scallops and wrap around the sides of the scallops. Prepare these a couple of hours ahead and refrigerate. Bring to room temperature about 20 minutes before grilling. If the sea scallops are really large, cut them in half.

1 lb. medium scallops, about 1- or 1½-inch diameter
grated rind (zest) from 1 lemon
2 tbs. fresh lemon juice

2 tsp. finely chopped fresh tarragon, or ½ tsp. dried
8 thin slices Danish ham, cut into 1-inch wide strips

Wash scallops and remove small muscle on side of scallop. Combine lemon zest, juice and tarragon in a small bowl and toss scallops with mixture. Wrap each scallop in a strip of ham, and thread on metal or presoaked wood skewers. Cook on a hot preheated grill for 2 to 3 minutes a side until scallops are opaque.

VARIATIONS

- Lightly spread ham slices with Dijon mustard before cutting into strips and wrapping around scallops, and substitute dried dill weed for the tarragon.
- Use thin strips of prosciutto in place of ham.

GRILLED SHRIMP
WITH COCKTAIL SAUCE

Grilled shrimp are always a party favorite. Dip them in a delicious sauce and double the recipe if you know your audience.

1 lb. large shrimp (20-25 per lb.), peeled, deveined
1 tbs. lemon juice
1 tbs. olive oil
1 recipe *European-Style Cocktail Sauce*, page 68, or *Tartar Sauce*, page 68

Arrange shrimp on metal or presoaked wood skewers, keeping shrimp slightly curled so the skewer goes through both the tail and thicker part of the body. Combine lemon juice and olive oil; brush shrimp with mixture. Cook shrimp on a preheated grill for about 4 to 5 minutes a side, until shrimp turn pink and are slightly firm to the touch. Serve immediately with dipping sauce.

GRILLED BREAD ROLL-UPS

Makes: 16

This recipe can be varied with any of the fillings on the following pages, and can be done well ahead for a party. Use your favorite combinations and be prepared for an encore. Be sure to buy the thinly sliced bread and roll it as flat as possible with a rolling pin.

8 thin slices bread
1 tbs. butter
1 tbs. olive oil
filling of choice, pages 25-28

Remove crusts from bread. Roll as thin as possible with a rolling pin. Melt butter and oil together. Brush both sides of bread with butter-oil mixture. Fill as directed with one of the filling recipes that immediately follow on pages 25-28. Carefully roll up into a tight roll. Cut each roll in half and arrange on a metal or presoaked wood skewer. Cover with a damp paper towel and refrigerate if not grilling immediately. Brush with more butter-oil mixture just before grilling. Grill over medium heat for about 2 minutes a side until bread is nicely browned and cheese is soft. Serve hot.

CHEESE AND SUN-DRIED TOMATO FILLING

For variety, substitute a thin slice of anchovy for the sun-dried tomatoes.

1 tbs. Dijon mustard
8 strips Swiss, Gruyère or cheddar cheese, about ½-inch wide x ½-inch thick x 4
   inches long
8 oil-packed, sun-dried tomatoes, cut into thin strips

Brush a thin layer of mustard on one side of bread. Place cheese strips close to one edge with sun-dried tomato slices on each side of cheese. Tightly roll up bread around filling. Grill as directed.

BLACK OLIVE AND GOAT CHEESE FILLING

1-2 tbs. black olive paste
⅓-½ cup creamy goat cheese
8 strips roasted red bell peppers

Spread bread slices on one side with a thin layer of black olive paste and top with a layer of goat cheese. Place a red pepper strip close to one edge of bread and tightly roll up bread around filling. Grill as directed.

HAM AND CHEESE FILLING

8 thin slices Danish-style ham
8 strips Monterey Jack or smoked Gouda cheese, about ½-inch wide x ½-inch
  thick x 4 inches long
8 strips roasted red bell peppers or thinly sliced dill pickle

Top bread slices with ham, strips of cheese and red peppers or pickle. Tightly roll up bread around filling. Grill as directed.

ASPARAGUS AND CHEESE FILLING

1-2 tbs. Dijon mustard
4-6 tbs. light cream cheese or goat cheese
8 cooked asparagus spears, about 4 inches long
¼ cup grated Parmesan cheese

Lightly spread bread slices with mustard, followed by a thin layer of cream cheese. Top with an asparagus spear, sprinkle with Parmesan cheese and tightly roll up bread around filling. Grill as directed.

EGGPLANT AND RED PEPPER FILLING

4-6 tbs. herbed cream cheese or goat cheese
16 slices grilled Japanese eggplant
16 strips roasted red bell peppers
1-2 tsp. drained, rinsed capers

Lightly spread bread slices with cream cheese. Top with 2 small slices eggplant and 2 strips roasted peppers. Sprinkle with a few capers. Tightly roll up bread around filling. Grill as directed.

GREEN CHILE AND HOT PEPPER CHEESE FILLING

4-6 tbs. light cream cheese
2-3 canned green chiles, or roasted fresh, peeled chiles
8 strips hot pepper Jack cheese, about ½-inch wide x ½-inch thick x 4 inches long

Lightly spread bread slices with light cream cheese. Cut green chiles into long ½-inch-wide strips. Place 2 strips chile and 1 strip hot pepper cheese on bread. Tightly roll up bread around filling. Grill as directed.

SMOKED SALMON AND LEEK FILLING

2 small leeks
2 tsp. butter
4-6 tbs. light cream cheese
8 strips smoked salmon, about 1 inch wide x 4 inches long
freshly ground pepper

Use white part of leeks, cut in half lengthwise and wash well to remove any sand. Cut into thin half-round slices. Sauté leeks in butter for 5 to 6 minutes until soft. Remove from heat and cool slightly. Spread bread slices with light cream cheese, top with salmon strips and scatter cooked leeks on top of salmon. Tightly roll up bread around filling. Grill as directed.

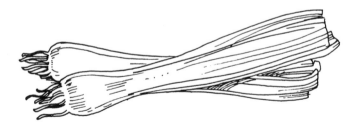

GRILLED OKRA WITH THAI DIPPING SAUCE

Lightly grilled okra is delicious dipped into a spicy Thai sauce or pesto.

20 okra pods
full-flavored olive oil
salt

Trim stem ends of okra. Pour a little olive oil and salt in a plate and toss okra to coat. Thread okra on metal or presoaked wood skewers and grill over medium heat for 10 to 12 minutes, turning frequently, or until okra softens and is lightly browned. Serve with *Thai Dipping Sauce*.

THAI DIPPING SAUCE

¼ cup rice wine vinegar
¼ cup sugar
dash salt
dash red pepper flakes

1 tbs. finely chopped peeled, seeded cucumber
1 tbs. finely chopped fresh cilantro leaves

Combine vinegar, sugar, salt and red pepper flakes in a small saucepan. Bring to a boil. Remove from heat, cool, and add chopped cucumber and cilantro.

CRAB AND ARTICHOKE HEART SKEWERS

Servings: 4-6

Here is another quick appetizer using imitation pink crab logs found in the supermarket refrigerator case. They are fully cooked and just need a little warming. Alternate on skewers with cooked artichoke hearts. Dip into **Romesco Dip***, page 21.*

1 pkg. (8 oz.) imitation crabmeat logs
1 can (8½ oz.) artichoke hearts, or 1 pkg. frozen, defrosted
1 tbs. olive oil

Cut each crabmeat log into 3 pieces. Drain and rinse artichoke hearts under cold water and cut each in half. Alternate crab and artichoke pieces on metal or presoaked wood skewers. Brush with olive oil and grill over medium heat for about 2 to 3 minutes a side, or until crab and artichokes are hot.

VARIATION

- Marinate artichoke hearts and fresh small mushrooms in Italian-style salad dressing before grilling.

YAKITORI

This tasty favorite can be put together ahead of time and refrigerated in the marinade. Be sure to soak the wood skewers before threading on the chicken.

1/3 cup soy sauce
2 tbs. mirin (Japanese rice wine)
2 tbs. dry sherry
1 tbs. minced ginger root
1/4 cup sugar

1/2 lb. boneless, skinless chicken breast
5-6 green onions, white part only, cut
  into 1-inch pieces
toasted sesame seeds for garnish

Combine soy sauce, mirin, dry sherry, ginger and sugar in a small saucepan and bring to a boil. Boil for 2 minutes, stirring to dissolve sugar, and strain into a small bowl. Let marinade cool to room temperature before pouring over chicken. Cut chicken into 1-inch cubes and marinate for 10 to 15 minutes, or cover with marinade and refrigerate for 1 to 2 hours. Alternate chicken and green onions on skewers and grill over medium heat for 4 to 5 minutes each side. Turn frequently and brush with marinade several times. Brush with marinade again just before serving and sprinkle with toasted sesame seeds.

GRILLED POULTRY SKEWER MEALS

Grilling is a particularly delicious and healthful way to prepare chicken and turkey. Marinades with fresh herbs, spices, yogurt, lemon or orange juice paired with light or dark meat, as you prefer, provide a wonderful variety of easily prepared entrées.

Removing the skin is optional. We tend to remove it before grilling because we like skin only when it is very crisp, and grilling doesn't always produce this result. Leaving the skin on does help baste the meat and keep it more moist, but marinades also will provide moisture.

It is important to take precautions when working with poultry. The meat should be kept cold and washed in cold water. Cutting boards and knives should be thoroughly cleaned in hot soapy water when you have finished. Cut the meat into similar-sized pieces for even cooking, and place it in the refrigerator if marinating for longer than 20 to 30 minutes.

For quick, easy grilled entrées, try *Mustard-Glazed Chicken on Rosemary Skewers*, *Indonesian Turkey Satay with Peanut Sauce* or *Grilled Chicken Kabobs with Tomatillo Sauce*. If you like spicy flavors, make the smoky *Chipotle Chile Chicken* with a savory *Avocado Salsa*, or West Indies-style *Jamaican Jerked Chicken and Plantains* with traditional *Rice and Peas*. Some substantial one-dish dinners include *Grilled Chicken Burritos*, and *Chorizo and Chicken with Rice Casserole*. We include many ideas and recipes for dishes to serve with these delicious grilled birds. Two of our favorites are *Tuscan-Style Beans* and *Sun-Dried Tomato Couscous*.

It's time to get out the grill!

GRILLED CHICKEN BURRITOS

Servings: 3-4

Grilled strips of chicken and a savory bean salad are rolled into large hot flour tortillas for a delicious dinner. Use fresh salsa from the deli or make your own, but it should be spicy. Try this same combination with chunks of grilled firm fresh fish. Let each person fill his own burrito.

4 boneless, skinless chicken breasts
1 tbs. vegetable oil
½ tsp. ground cumin
1 can (15 oz.) black beans, drained
1 can (11 oz.) whole kernel corn, drained
½ cup prepared hot fresh tomato salsa

⅓ cup light sour cream
1 tbs. Dijon mustard
salt and freshly ground pepper
4-6 large flour tortillas, about 9-inch diameter
fresh cilantro leaves for garnish

Cut each chicken breast lengthwise into 3 equal strips and thread on metal or presoaked wood skewers. Combine vegetable oil and cumin and brush over chicken strips. Pour beans and corn into a colander, rinse with cold water and drain well. Pour into a mixing bowl. Add salsa, sour cream, mustard, salt and pepper; mix well. Wrap flour tortillas in foil and heat in a 350° oven for 10 minutes. Grill chicken on a preheated grill for about 3 to 4 minutes a side. Spread ⅓ to ½ cup bean mixture on lower third of hot tortilla. Top with chicken strips and cilantro leaves. Roll up and eat out of hand.

POLYNESIAN PINEAPPLE CHICKEN

Servings: 3-4

*Alternate chicken with pineapple chunks. Serve with **Pineapple Rice**, page 37; asparagus or broccoli adds a nice color touch.*

1½ lb. boneless, skinless chicken thighs, about 6

MARINADE
⅓ cup soy sauce
¼ cup sugar

2 tbs. vegetable oil
½ tsp. grated ginger root

GARNISH
fresh or canned pineapple chunks
1 large green bell pepper, seeded, cut into 1½-inch squares

Cut thighs into 2 or 3 pieces of similar size. Wash and dry chicken. Combine marinade ingredients, pour into a plastic bag, or glass or stainless steel bowl, and add chicken pieces. Marinate in the refrigerator for about 3 hours. Remove chicken from marinade. Arrange chicken pieces on metal or presoaked wood skewers, alternating pineapple chunks and green pepper pieces with chicken. Brush chicken skewers with marinade once or twice during grilling. Cook for 8 to 10 minutes a side on a preheated grill until chicken is done.

PINEAPPLE RICE

If you are serving rice lovers, this recipe can be easily doubled.

1 can (7 oz.) unsweetened pineapple chunks with juice
1 can (14½ oz.) chicken broth
1 tbs. butter
dash salt
freshly ground pepper
a few drops Tabasco Sauce
1 cup uncooked long-grain rice

Drain juice from pineapple into a measuring cup and add enough chicken broth to make 1¾ cups liquid. Pour into a medium saucepan and add butter, salt, pepper and Tabasco. Bring to a rapid boil. Add rice and pineapple chunks, bring back to a boil, cover and turn heat to lowest setting. Cook for 15 minutes, lift lid and fluff rice with a fork. Replace lid and continue to cook over low heat for 3 minutes. Remove pan from heat and allow to steam without lifting lid for 10 minutes. Serve hot.

MUSTARD-GLAZED CHICKEN ON ROSEMARY SKEWERS

Servings: 2-3

*If you have a large rosemary bush in your herb garden, or find a large bunch in the market, select 3 or 4 of the larger, longer branches and remove the needles. Soak branches in water for 20 minutes before using to skewer the chicken pieces. Or use metal or presoaked wood skewers. Serve with **Tuscan-Style Bread Salad**, page 39.*

1 lb. boneless, skinless chicken thighs
5-6 green onions, trimmed, white part and about 1 inch of green

MARINADE
1 tbs. full-flavored olive oil
2 tbs. stone-ground mustard
2 tbs. vermouth

1 tsp. brown sugar
½ tsp. Tabasco Jalapeño Sauce
salt and freshly ground pepper

Cut chicken thighs into 2 or 3 pieces of similar size. Wash and dry chicken. Combine marinade ingredients and pour over chicken. Marinate for 30 minutes. Alternate chicken pieces on presoaked rosemary skewers or metal skewers with green onion pieces. Cook on a preheated grill for 10 to 12 minutes a side until chicken is done.

TUSCAN-STYLE BREAD SALAD

Servings: 2-3

Use day-old French or Italian bread cut into 1-inch-thick slices to make this delicious grilled salad. Put the salad together and allow it to stand while the chicken or meat is grilling.

6 thick slices bread, crusts removed, cut into 1-inch cubes
1 large sweet red or white onion, cut into ½-inch slices
1-2 tbs. full-flavored olive oil
2 tbs. dried currants
1 tbs. balsamic vinegar
2 large ripe tomatoes, peeled, seeded, diced

2 tbs. toasted pine nuts
10-12 fresh basil leaves, cut into ribbons
2 tbs. chicken broth
1 tbs. full-flavored olive oil
2 tsp. white wine vinegar
salt and freshly ground pepper
a few leaves of arugula or torn lettuce leaves

Thread bread cubes and onion slices on skewers, brush with 1 tbs. olive oil and grill until lightly browned. While bread and onions are grilling, soak currants in balsamic vinegar. Place toasted bread cubes in a bowl. Cut onion into ½-inch pieces, and add to bread with tomato, soaked currants, pine nuts and basil leaves. Whisk together chicken broth, olive oil, vinegar, salt and pepper and toss mixture with bread cubes. Line a platter with arugula or lettuce leaves and top with bread salad.

CHIPOTLE CHILE CHICKEN

*If you love chiles, this dish is for you. Use part of a small can of chipotle peppers in adobo sauce. Serve chicken in hot flour tortillas with **Avocado Salsa**, page 41. Or make a fresh pineapple, orange and avocado salad and cook some couscous or rice to complement the spicy chicken. This recipe doubles easily.*

3 boneless, skinless chicken breasts, each cut into 3 pieces

MARINADE
1 canned chipotle chile
2 tbs. adobo sauce
1 tbs. lime juice
1 tbs. vegetable oil
½ tsp. ground cumin
¼ tsp. dried oregano

Arrange chicken pieces on metal or presoaked wood skewers. Combine marinade ingredients in a blender container and process until smooth. Brush all sides of chicken with marinade and let stand for 20 to 30 minutes. Brush again with marinade. Cook on a preheated grill for 12 to 14 minutes, turning once or twice, until chicken is done.

AVOCADO SALSA

*Spoon this salsa into hot tortillas with some spicy **Chipotle Chile Chicken**. It also is delicious when scooped up with crispy tortilla chips. If you double the recipe, use 1 tbs. lime juice.*

1 large avocado, peeled, cut into ½-inch chunks
1 medium-sized ripe tomato, peeled, seeded, chopped
3 green onions, finely chopped
2 tsp. fresh lime juice
salt and freshly ground pepper
½ tsp. Tabasco Jalapeño Sauce
2-3 tbs. coarsely chopped cilantro

Combine ingredients in a small bowl and mix lightly, taking care not to smash the avocado. Let stand for 15 to 20 minutes to allow the flavors to combine.

CHICKEN WITH YOGURT MINT MARINADE

Servings: 2-3

*Accompany these savory chicken breast skewers with **Herbed Pilaf**, page 43. Or tuck into warm pita breads with pieces of cucumber and tomato moistened with a little more yogurt and fresh cilantro leaves.*

3-4 boneless, skinless chicken breasts
2 cloves garlic, peeled, coarsely
  chopped
1 tsp. grated ginger root
4 green onions, white part only, cut into
  ½-inch pieces
1 tbs. vegetable oil
1 tsp. paprika

1 tsp. ground cumin
grated rind (zest) from 1 lime
1 tbs. fresh lime juice
½ tsp. salt
1 tsp. dried mint, or 1 tbs. chopped
  fresh
dash red pepper flakes
1 cup plain yogurt

Cut each chicken breast lengthwise into 3 pieces. Combine remaining ingredients in a blender or food processor bowl and process until almost smooth. Pour marinade over chicken strips and marinate in the refrigerator for 2 to 3 hours. Thread chicken strips on metal or presoaked wood skewers. Grill over medium high heat for 3 to 4 minutes each side, turning once.

HERBED PILAF

Try this flavorful pilaf with grilled chicken or fish dishes. If you wish, replace part of the broth with coconut milk.

1 tbs. butter
1 tbs. light olive oil
1 small jalapeño pepper, seeded, finely
  chopped
½ cup finely chopped onion
1 cup uncooked long-grain rice
½ cup diced uncooked potato

1 tbs. lemon juice
1¾ cups chicken or vegetable broth
½ tsp. salt
½ cup green peas
½ tsp. dried marjoram
2 tbs. chopped fresh parsley
2 tbs. chopped fresh mint leaves

Heat butter and oil in a heavy saucepan and sauté jalapeño pepper and onion for 5 to 6 minutes until onion is soft but not brown. Stir in rice and diced potato, toss with onion mixture and continue to cook until rice grains turn slightly translucent. Add lemon juice, chicken broth and salt; cover and cook over very low heat for about 18 minutes until rice is tender and liquid has been absorbed. Stir in peas and marjoram, cover and cook for 3 to 4 more minutes until peas are done. Stir in fresh parsley and mint leaves.

SKEWERED CHICKEN BALSAMICO

Servings: 2-3

*Balsamic vinegar adds a wonderful flavor to marinades. Serve this grilled chicken with **Sun-Dried Tomato Couscous**, page 45, and sugar snap peas.*

3-4 boneless, skinless chicken breasts
1/4 cup full-flavored olive oil
3 tbs. balsamic vinegar
1 large clove garlic, peeled, coarsely chopped
1 medium shallot, peeled, coarsely sliced
1/4 tsp. salt
1/4 tsp. freshly ground pepper
1/2 tsp. dried oregano
1/4 tsp. red pepper flakes

Cut each chicken breast lengthwise into 3 equal strips and place in a shallow stainless or glass bowl. Combine remaining ingredients in a blender container and process until smooth. Pour mixture over chicken and allow to marinate for 30 to 40 minutes in the refrigerator. Thread chicken pieces on metal or presoaked wood skewers. Cook on a preheated grill for about 3 to 4 minutes a side; baste 2 or 3 times with marinade during cooking.

SUN-DRIED TOMATO COUSCOUS

Servings: 3-4

Couscous cooks in 5 minutes and is a wonderful foil for many different herbs and seasonings.

¾ cup water or chicken broth
1 tbs. full-flavored olive oil
½ cup quick-cooking couscous
salt and freshly ground pepper
½ tsp. finely chopped fresh thyme or oregano leaves
10-12 oil-packed sun-dried tomatoes, chopped
3 tbs. toasted pine nuts

Combine water and olive oil in a medium skillet and bring to a boil. Add couscous, salt, pepper and thyme. Cover, remove from heat and allow to stand for 5 minutes. Remove cover, fluff grains with a fork and stir in sun-dried tomatoes and pine nuts.

CHORIZO AND CHICKEN WITH RICE

Servings: 4-6

This hearty dish combines grilled homemade turkey chorizo sausages and chunks of grilled chicken with a savory rice casserole. Cook rice first, and then grill the chorizo and chicken. A spatula helps to turn the meatballs over on the grill.

CHORIZO

½ lb. ground turkey
1 tbs. chili powder
⅛ tsp. ground coriander
¼ tsp. garlic powder
1 tbs. cracker crumbs

1 tbs. red wine vinegar
1 egg white, unbeaten
salt and freshly ground pepper
olive oil for brushing

Combine turkey with chile powder, coriander, garlic powder, cracker crumbs and vinegar; mix well. Combine egg white with salt and pepper and stir into meat. Form into 9 equal meatballs. Cover and refrigerate for about 1 hour. Arrange on metal or presoaked wood skewers. Brush with olive oil. Grill on a preheated grill for about 10 to 14 minutes, turning often, until nicely browned and firm to the touch.

GRILLED CHICKEN

4 boneless, skinless chicken thighs
2 tsp. lemon juice

2 tsp. olive oil
salt and freshly ground pepper

Cut each chicken thigh into 3 pieces and arrange on metal or presoaked wood skewer. Brush with lemon juice and olive oil; season with salt and pepper. Grill on a preheated grill for about 8 to 10 minutes a side, or until chicken is firm to the touch and no longer pink.

RICE CASSEROLE

1 can (6½ oz.) chopped clams
1 bottle (8 oz.) clam juice
water as necessary
3 tbs. full-flavored olive oil
½ cup chopped onion
dash red pepper flakes

1½ cups uncooked long-grain rice
2 large cloves garlic, finely chopped
2 tbs. finely chopped fresh parsley
1 large tomato, peeled, seeded, diced
½ tsp. salt
freshly ground pepper

Drain clams and reserve juice. Combine reserved clam juice with bottled clam juice, plus enough water to make 2¾ cups total liquid; set aside. Heat olive oil in large heavy skillet. Sauté onion for 5 to 6 minutes until soft. Stir in red pepper flakes and rice. Stir to coat with oil and cook for 2 to 3 minutes until rice becomes translucent. Add remaining ingredients and clam liquid; bring to a rapid boil. Cover tightly and reduce heat to barest simmer. Cook for 18 minutes without lifting lid. Stir in clams. Check rice to see if it is tender and add ¼ cup additional water if rice is not done. Cook covered for a few more minutes. Serve rice with chorizo and chicken on the side.

BUTTERMILK-MARINATED CHICKEN KABOBS

*Try this easy, lightly spicy buttermilk marinade. The buttermilk tenderizes the chicken. Serve with **Black Bean and Salsa Salad**, page 117, or potato salad, and a platter of marinated vegetables.*

1 lb. boneless, skinless chicken thighs
⅔ cup buttermilk
1 tsp. Tabasco Jalapeño Sauce
1 tsp. paprika
salt and freshly ground pepper

Cut each chicken thigh into 2 or 3 equal pieces. Combine remaining ingredients and marinate chicken in the refrigerator for 2 to 3 hours. Thread chicken pieces on metal or presoaked wood skewers. Grill over medium heat for 10 to 12 minutes a side, until chicken is no longer pink and is firm to the touch.

LEMON MUSTARD CHICKEN

Servings: 2-3

Fresh herbs and mustard make a savory marinade. Use a combination of your favorite fresh herbs and change them with the seasons.

1 lb. boneless, skinless chicken breasts
1 tbs. olive oil
grated rind (zest) from 1 lemon
1 tbs. fresh lemon juice
½ tsp. grated ginger root
1 tbs. Dijon mustard
2 tbs. minced fresh herbs (parsley, mint, thyme, basil, tarragon)
freshly ground pepper

Cut each chicken breast lengthwise into 3 pieces. Thread chicken on metal or presoaked wood skewers. Brush with a little olive oil. Combine remaining ingredients. Grill chicken on a preheated grill for about 3 to 4 minutes a side, turning once or twice. Brush chicken with herb-mustard mixture each time chicken is turned. Cook until chicken springs back lightly to the touch.

GRILLED CHICKEN KABOBS
WITH TOMATILLO SAUCE

Servings: 2-3

Grilled chicken is topped with a piquant Mexican tomatillo sauce, which can be made ahead and served hot or at room temperature. Tomatillo sauce complements fish as well and also doubles as a delicious dip for crisp tortilla chips.

1 lb. boneless, skinless chicken thighs

MARINADE
1 tbs. olive oil
a few drops lime juice
1/4 tsp. cumin
salt and pepper

Cut chicken thighs into 2 or 3 pieces of similar size. Wash and dry chicken. Combine marinade ingredients and rub into chicken pieces. Thread chicken on metal or presoaked wood skewers. Cook on a preheated grill for 8 to 10 minutes a side, until chicken is done. Serve with *Tomatillo Sauce*.

TOMATILLO SAUCE

1 can (12 oz.) tomatillos, drained
1 fresh jalapeño chile, stemmed, seeded, chopped
1 clove garlic, chopped
1/4 cup chopped onion
1/2 cup loosely packed cilantro leaves
salt and freshly ground pepper
1 tbs. vegetable oil

Combine sauce ingredients, except vegetable oil, in a food processor bowl and process until texture is fairly smooth. Heat vegetable oil in a small saucepan, stir in sauce and cook over medium heat for about 5 minutes. Spoon over grilled chicken.

JAMAICAN JERKED CHICKEN AND PLANTAINS

Servings: 4-6

*Serve this with a typical West Indian dish of **Rice and Peas**, page 53, and grilled plantains. Plantains should be very ripe, with almost black peel.*

½ cup coarsely chopped onion
2 tsp. dried thyme
2 tsp. allspice
½ tsp. cinnamon
⅛ tsp. freshly grated nutmeg
2 tsp. salt

freshly ground black pepper
¼ tsp. cayenne pepper, or to taste
1 tbs. vegetable oil
6 boneless, skinless chicken thighs
2 ripe plantains
oil for brushing plantains

Place onion, seasonings and 1 tbs. vegetable oil in a food processor bowl and process until mixture forms a smooth paste. Rub chicken well with marinade mixture and refrigerate for 1 hour. Skewer thighs on double skewers, maintaining as uniform a thickness as possible. Peel plantains and cut each into 6 pieces, cutting slices at an angle. With your palm, smash slices to about a ½-inch thickness. Thread slices on skewers and brush with oil. Grill chicken and plantains over hot coals for about 8 to 10 minutes a side, or until chicken is firm to the touch and no longer pink. Serve hot.

RICE AND PEAS

This is a typical West Indian dish of rice, red beans and coconut milk. The red kidney beans are known as "peas." The coconut milk is essential to provide authentic texture and flavor. Canned coconut milk is available in most food markets in the Asian, Thai or Chinese sections, and there is a "light" version now on the shelves.

2 tbs. vegetable oil
1 medium onion, finely chopped
2 small fresh chile peppers, seeded, finely chopped
$\frac{1}{2}$ cup coconut milk
1 can (15$\frac{1}{4}$ oz.) red kidney beans, liquid reserved
water as necessary
1 cup uncooked rice
$\frac{1}{4}$ tsp. dried thyme
salt and freshly ground pepper

Heat oil in a large saucepan; sauté onion and peppers until soft but not brown. Pour coconut milk and bean liquid into a 2-cup measuring cup. Add enough water to make 2 cups liquid; pour liquid into saucepan. Add rice, thyme, salt and pepper. Bring to a boil, cover and simmer over very low heat for 20 to 25 minutes until rice is cooked. Stir in kidney beans and cook for another 5 minutes.

CHICKEN KABOBS WITH PIQUANT PARSLEY SAUCE

*Grilled chicken is served with a lively green typical Italian sauce. Small **Grilled New Potatoes**, page 155, make a great accompaniment and are delicious drizzled with some of the sauce. Try this sauce with grilled fish, too.*

6 boneless, skinless chicken thighs
1 tbs. lemon juice mixed with 1 tbs. olive oil

Cut each chicken thigh into 3 equal pieces and arrange on metal or presoaked wood skewers. Brush chicken pieces with lemon juice-oil mixture and grill for about 10 to 12 minutes a side or until chicken is no longer pink and is firm to the touch. Spoon *Parsley Sauce* over chicken.

PARSLEY SAUCE

1/2 cup loosely packed fresh Italian parsley
1 clove garlic, peeled, chopped
1 small shallot, peeled, chopped
1 tbs. rinsed, drained capers
1/2 tsp. anchovy paste

1/2 tsp. Dijon mustard
1 1/2 tbs. lemon juice
1/3 cup full-flavored olive oil
salt and freshly ground pepper

With a food processor, finely chop parsley, garlic and shallot. Add remaining ingredients and process until mixture is well combined but not completely smooth.

SPICY TURKEY KABOBS BOMBAY

Yogurt spiced with cumin, coriander and ginger gives an East Indian flavor to marinated grilled turkey. Serve with a sliced orange and red onion salad and tiny new potatoes.

2 whole turkey tenderloins (1¼ lb.)
1 cup plain yogurt
1 tbs. lime juice
1 tbs. vegetable oil
⅓ cup coarsely chopped onion
1 tsp. grated ginger root
2 tsp. ground cumin

½ tsp. dry mustard
½ tsp. ground coriander
¼ tsp. allspice
¼ tsp. ground cardamom
¼ tsp. red pepper flakes
freshly ground pepper
2 tbs. fresh cilantro leaves

Cut turkey tenderloins in half lengthwise. Remove central tendon and silvery skin. Cut into 1½-inch chunks and place in a glass or stainless steel bowl. Put remaining ingredients in a blender container or food processor bowl. Process until smooth. Pour over turkey chunks and marinate in the refrigerator for 2 to 3 hours. Remove from refrigerator about 30 minutes before cooking. Thread on skewers, place on a pre-heated grill and cook for 10 to 12 minutes until firm to the touch and no longer pink.

TERIYAKI TURKEY KABOBS

Buy a half turkey breast piece and cut into chunks for grilling. Serve with **Gingered Noodle Salad**, *page 57, and some cooked zucchini or yellow squash.*

MARINADE

2 tbs. soy sauce
2 tbs. lemon juice
2 tbs. vegetable oil
1 tsp. sesame oil

1 clove garlic, minced
1 tsp. minced ginger root
dash red pepper flakes

1 lb. boneless, skinless turkey breast, cut into 1½-inch cubes
6-8 green onions, white part with about 1 inch of green

Combine marinade ingredients and pour over turkey pieces. Marinate for about 30 minutes. Remove from marinade. Cut green onions into 1½- to 2-inch pieces. Alternate turkey cubes with green onions on metal or presoaked wood skewers. Cook on a preheated grill for about 12 to 15 minutes, turning once or twice, until turkey is cooked through and slightly firm to the touch. Brush several times with marinade while grilling.

GINGERED NOODLE SALAD

*Serve with **Teriyaki Turkey Kabobs**, page 56, or **Beef and Mushroom Teriyaki**, page 119. This salad is also delicious with a few cooked shrimp or chicken chunks.*

8 oz. fresh Asian-style noodles or 6 oz. dried spaghettini
2 tbs. peanut oil
1 small carrot, coarsely grated
6-8 snow peas, blanched for 1 minute, cut into thin strips

3 green onions, white part only, cut into thin strips
Dressing, follows
salt and freshly ground pepper
toasted sesame seeds and fresh cilantro leaves

Cook pasta according to package directions. Rinse under cold water and drain. Place in a large bowl and immediately toss with peanut oil. Add vegetable strips to pasta. Pour dressing over vegetables and pasta and lightly toss salad with two forks. Add salt and pepper. Chill in the refrigerator for about 1 hour and toss with sesame seeds and cilantro leaves before serving.

DRESSING

2 tbs. rice wine vinegar, or cider vinegar
1 tsp. sesame oil
1 tbs. light soy sauce

1 tsp. finely grated ginger root
½ tsp. Tabasco Jalapeño Sauce
dash red pepper flakes, or to taste

Combine ingredients.

TURKEY APPLE KABOBS

Servings: 3-4

*Turkey breast pieces are marinated in apple juice and grilled with apple chunks. Serve with baked sweet potatoes and **Cranberry Kiwi Relish**, page 59.*

1 lb. boneless, skinless turkey breast, cut into 1½-inch cubes
1 cup apple juice
½ tsp. Tabasco Jalapeño Sauce

2 large Golden Delicious apples
2 tsp. Dijon mustard
2 tbs. apple jelly
salt and freshly ground pepper

Place turkey pieces in a glass or stainless steel bowl and pour apple juice and Tabasco over turkey. Cover and marinate in the refrigerator for about 1 hour. Core apples, cut in half vertically and horizontally, and then cut each quarter in half to yield 8 equal pieces. Remove turkey from marinade and place remaining marinade in a small saucepan. Alternate turkey and apple pieces on metal or presoaked wood skewers. Grill over medium heat for about 12 to 15 minutes, or until turkey is done and slightly firm to the touch. While turkey is grilling, bring marinade to a boil and reduce over high heat for about 5 minutes. Lower heat and stir in mustard, jelly, salt and pepper. During the last 5 minutes of grilling, brush kabobs 2 or 3 times with marinade. Brush kabobs generously with marinade just before serving.

CRANBERRY KIWI RELISH

Makes: 2 cups

Cranberries paired with kiwi make a zesty accent for grilled chicken or turkey dishes. Make at least 2 hours ahead so flavors can blend.

1 cup fresh or frozen cranberries, picked over and washed
2 kiwi, peeled, cut into quarters
3 tbs. sugar
2 tbs. frozen orange juice concentrate

Place cranberries with remaining ingredients in a food processor and process until mixture is well combined but still has some texture. Refrigerate until ready to serve.

GRILLED TURKEY KABOBS HAWAIIAN

Servings: 4

*Island flavors of rum, lime juice and honey make a quick marinade for turkey. Serve with **Pineapple Rice**, page 37, or **Orange Almond Rice Pilaf**, page 75, and a crunchy green vegetable. Or make a big fruit salad and serve with crisp baked potato wedges.*

2 turkey tenderloins (1¼ lb.)
3 tbs. honey
1 tbs. Dijon mustard
3 tbs. dark rum
¼ cup lime juice
1 tbs. brown sugar
1 tbs. vegetable oil

Cut tenderloins in half lengthwise. Remove the central tendon and silvery skin. Cut into 1½-inch chunks and place in a glass or stainless steel bowl. Combine remaining ingredients and pour over turkey pieces. Marinate for 20 to 30 minutes at room temperature. Arrange turkey chunks on metal or presoaked wood skewers. Cook on a preheated grill for about 10 to 12 minutes, until turkey is nicely browned and firm to the touch.

INDONESIAN TURKEY SATAY
WITH PEANUT SAUCE

Wrap these turkey chunks in crisp lettuce leaves, or tuck them into pita pockets, and spoon the peanut sauce over them, for an informal summer lunch or hot summer night dinner. Serve with fresh pineapple or melon slices.

1 lb. boneless, skinless turkey breast,
  cut into 1-inch cubes
1 tbs. vegetable oil
1 small clove garlic, minced
½ tsp. grated ginger root
2 green onions, white part only, finely
  chopped
½ cup chicken broth

3 tbs. peanut butter
1 tbs. soy sauce
2 tsp. brown sugar
dash red pepper flakes
1 tsp. cider vinegar
2 tbs. dried currants
fresh cilantro leaves for garnish

Arrange turkey cubes on metal or presoaked wood skewers and brush with vegetable oil. Combine remaining ingredients, except cilantro, in a small saucepan. Bring to a boil and cook for 2 to 3 minutes. Let mixture cool while turkey is grilling. Cook turkey on a preheated grill for 8 to 10 minutes, until turkey is nicely browned and slightly firm to the touch. Remove from skewers and serve with peanut sauce and fresh cilantro leaves.

GRILLED ITALIAN-STYLE TURKEY SAUSAGES

Servings: 2-3

*These delicious homemade sausages are perfect with **Tuscan-Style Beans**, page 63, or put them into sandwiches with some grilled peppers. These are a little fragile, so you will find a spatula helpful in rolling them over on the grill.*

1 lb. ground dark turkey meat
1 tsp. crushed fennel seeds
½ tsp. red pepper flakes
½ tsp. salt
½ tsp. freshly ground pepper
1 clove garlic, finely minced
1 egg white
olive oil for brushing

Place turkey meat in a mixing bowl, add spices and garlic, and blend with a fork until well combined. Stir egg white into meat. Form into 16 equal balls. Refrigerate for at least 1 hour. Arrange sausages on metal or presoaked wood skewers and brush with olive oil. Cook on a preheated grill for 6 to 8 minutes a side, or until sausage is nicely browned and firm to the touch. Serve immediately.

TUSCAN-STYLE BEANS

This is a great accompaniment to many grilled chicken and meat dishes. Serve at room temperature or warm slightly in the microwave. The recipe can be easily doubled, and it can also be made ahead and refrigerated. Add a couple of table-spoons of chopped roasted red peppers or a peeled, seeded, chopped ripe tomato for variation.

1¾ cups cooked or 1 can (15 oz.) small white beans
1 tbs. extra virgin olive oil
1 clove garlic, finely chopped
dash red pepper flakes
1 tsp. balsamic vinegar
salt and freshly ground pepper
2-3 fresh sage leaves, finely chopped, or 1 tbs. chopped fresh basil leaves

Drain beans in a sieve and rinse well with cold water. Allow to drain while preparing the rest of the dish. Combine olive oil, chopped garlic and pepper flakes in a small skillet. Sauté gently over low heat for 1 to 2 minutes just to soften garlic. Pour beans into a serving bowl; add garlic mixture and remaining ingredients. Mix well and serve. If refrigerated after preparing, remove from refrigerator about 30 minutes ahead and stir in fresh sage or basil leaves just before serving.

GRILLED SEAFOOD SKEWER MEALS

Grilling is a delicious, healthful way to prepare seafood. Grilled shrimp and scallops are always popular with shellfish lovers, and firm white fish like rock cod, red snapper, halibut or monkfish make marvelous entrées. Softer fish are cooked on the grill with grape leaf or lettuce leaf wraps.

HELPFUL TIPS FOR GRILLING SEAFOOD

- Be sure to oil the grill rack before cooking seafood to minimize sticking.

- For easier handling of seafood, use a double skewer or two parallel skewers. The fish tends to roll on a single skewer. Flat-sided skewers also keep food in place. Skewer shrimp by forming them in a rough circle, and threading them with the skewer in two places, one near the tail and again near the head.

- Use nonstick cooking spray to lightly coat seafood before grilling.

- Grill seafood over medium high heat so the outside gets browned but not charred.

- Long-handled spatulas, tongs and basting brushes are very useful to keep your distance from the fire. If you have an abundance of herbs, tie some to the end of your basting brush and use to brush more marinade on the grilling fish.

- Seafood should be turned only once during grilling, and we use "60/40" timing, which uses about 60 percent of the grilling time for cooking the first side, and 40 percent for the second side. Poke the fish with your finger during the grilling to see how firm the fish is becoming — fish becomes firmer as it cooks.

- Softer fish such as sole, whiting and orange roughy are too delicate to skewer and grill by themselves, so wrap them in grape or lettuce leaves before grilling.

- Seafood marinades usually contain significant amounts of lemon or lime juice, which quickly "cook" the fish, turning it opaque or white around the edges, so we suggest marinating seafood for no more than 15 to 20 minutes to prevent altering the texture.

BASIC LEMON BUTTER
BASTING MARINADE

If you don't want to make a marinade, or if you want to add an extra flavor fillip to any grilled fish, just brush on a little of this lemon butter while the seafood is grilling. Combine ingredients in a small saucepan and heat until butter melts, or microwave for a few seconds.

grated rind (zest) from 1 lemon
1 tbs. fresh lemon juice
1 tbs. butter
1-2 drops Tabasco Sauce or Tabasco Jalapeño Sauce

AROMATIC BUTTER SAUCES

See pages 160 and 161 for quick sauces for grilled fish:

- *Orange Ginger Butter*
- *Lemon Mint Butter*
- *Sun-Dried Tomato Butter*
- *Tarragon Butter*

TARTAR SAUCE

Makes: about 1 cup

Try this piquant sauce with simply grilled shrimp, scallops or fish kabobs.

2 tbs. finely chopped dill pickle
1 tbs. rinsed, drained, chopped capers
1 tbs. finely minced green onion
2 tbs. finely chopped fresh parsley

1 tsp. Dijon mustard
1 tsp. white wine vinegar or lemon juice
2-3 drops Tabasco Sauce
1 cup mayonnaise

Combine ingredients, except mayonnaise. Add mixture to mayonnaise and stir to blend. Refrigerate for at least 1 hour to allow flavors to blend. Serve in individual small serving cups or a small bowl. Refrigerate until ready to serve.

EUROPEAN-STYLE COCKTAIL SAUCE

Makes: about 1 cup

This is another delicious sauce for seafood that has been grilled without a strong marinade. Try it with cracked crab, or a crab and shrimp salad, too.

1 tbs. cognac or brandy
1 tbs. chili sauce or tomato paste
1 tbs. lemon juice

1 tsp. prepared horseradish
pinch white pepper
1 cup good quality mayonnaise

Whisk ingredients together, cover and refrigerate until ready to serve.

SCALLOPS IN SHALLOT AND SHERRY VINEGAR MARINADE

This flavorful marinade is terrific on shrimp, too. Use large 1½- to 2-inch sea scallops if they are available.

2 tsp. sherry wine vinegar
2 tsp. rice wine vinegar
grated rind (zest) from 1 lemon
2 tsp. fresh lemon juice

1 tbs. minced shallot
¼ cup olive oil
salt and freshly ground pepper
1 lb. large scallops

Place all ingredients, except scallops, in a small bowl and whisk until well combined. Wash scallops in several changes of water to remove any sand; take off small, tough muscle on side of scallop and discard. Place scallops in marinade and let stand for 15 to 20 minutes, turning occasionally. Thread scallops on two metal or presoaked wood skewers, for easier handling. Grill for about 5 minutes a side, turning once, until scallops are cooked and slightly firm to the touch. Brush scallops with marinade during grilling. Serve immediately.

SCALLOPS WITH LEMON CREAM PASTA

Servings: 4

Lemony angel hair pasta is superb with grilled scallops or shrimp. Italian purists would not serve cheese with seafood pasta dishes, but some finely grated Parmesan cheese is a delicious addition. After you prepare the scallops, make the sauce, and grill the scallops while the pasta is cooking.

1 lb. medium scallops
6 oz. dried angel hair or spaghettini pasta
2 tbs. finely chopped fresh parsley
grated Parmesan cheese, optional

MARINADE
2 tbs. butter
1 tbs. olive oil
1 clove garlic, minced

SAUCE
¼ cup dry vermouth or white wine
3 tbs. fresh lemon juice
2 tbs. finely chopped shallots
grated rind (zest) of 1 lemon

⅓ cup heavy cream
⅓ cup butter
salt and freshly ground pepper

Prepare scallops by washing thoroughly to remove any sand and pull off small muscle on side of scallops. Arrange scallops on metal or presoaked wood skewers.

To make marinade: Combine butter, olive oil and garlic in small microwavable dish and microwave for a few seconds to melt butter.

To make sauce: Combine vermouth, lemon juice and shallots in a medium skillet and cook over high heat until about 2 to 3 teaspoons of liquid remain. Add lemon zest and cream to pan, bring to a boil and cook for 2 to 3 minutes to reduce slightly. Reduce heat to very low and stir in butter 1 tbs. at a time, making sure butter is well incorporated in sauce before adding more. Sauce should be smooth and creamy.

Brush scallops with marinade and cook on a preheated grill for 3 to 4 minutes a side, turning once, until scallops are slightly firm to the touch.

Cook pasta according to package directions, drain well and add to skillet with sauce. Toss to combine hot pasta and sauce. Pour into a warm serving bowl or serve on individual warm plates. Sprinkle with chopped parsley and grated Parmesan if desired. Remove scallops from skewers and serve over hot pasta.

TERIYAKI SHRIMP

*This is a good marinade for scallops, too. Serve the hot grilled shrimp on a bed of **Napa Cabbage and Carrot Salad**, page 73.*

2 tbs. soy sauce
3 tbs. dry sherry or Shaoxing rice wine
1 tsp. brown sugar
1 tsp. sesame oil
½ lb. medium shrimp, peeled, deveined

Mix marinade ingredients together in a small bowl, add shrimp and marinate for 15 to 20 minutes. Arrange shrimp on metal or presoaked wood skewers and cook on a preheated grill for 3 to 4 minutes a side, turning once.

NAPA CABBAGE SALAD

Double this recipe if you are serving more people.

3 large carrots, peeled, coarsely grated (about 3 cups)
4 cups thinly sliced napa cabbage or regular cabbage
2 green onions, finely chopped
½ cup fresh cilantro leaves
Dressing, follows
1 tsp. toasted sesame seeds

Combine carrots, cabbage, onions and cilantro in a large bowl. Toss salad with dressing, sprinkle with sesame seeds and serve. If not serving immediately, refrigerate and sprinkle with sesame seeds just before serving.

DRESSING

2 tbs. vegetable oil
3 tbs. rice wine vinegar
1 tsp. sesame oil
1 tbs. lemon juice

1 tsp. sugar
¼ tsp. grated ginger root
dash red pepper flakes
salt and freshly ground pepper

Whisk together ingredients, stirring until sugar dissolves.

SHRIMP WITH ORANGE
AND LIME MARINADE

This bright citrus marinade is perfect for shrimp, scallops or chicken. Serve with **Orange Almond Rice Pilaf**, *page 75, and crisp green snow peas or broccoli.*

1 lb. medium shrimp, peeled, deveined

MARINADE
3 tbs. soy sauce
2 tbs. Shaoxing rice wine or dry sherry
2 tbs. lime juice
grated rind (zest) from 1 orange
2 tbs. fresh orange juice
1/4 tsp. grated ginger root

Combine shrimp with marinade and let stand for 20 minutes before grilling. Thread shrimp on skewers and cook on a preheated grill for 3 to 4 minutes a side, until shrimp turn pink and are firm to the touch.

ORANGE ALMOND RICE PILAF

Servings: 4

This delicately orange-flavored rice is a great accompaniment for seafood, turkey or pork dishes.

2 tbs. butter
1 medium onion, finely chopped
1 cup uncooked long-grain rice
grated rind (zest) from 1 orange
juice of 2 oranges, plus enough chicken broth to make 2 cups liquid
½ tsp. salt
¼ cup toasted slivered almonds
2 tbs. white raisins, optional

Melt butter in a large saucepan. Sauté onion until soft but not brown. Add rice to pan and stir until rice is well coated with butter and turns a milky or translucent color, about 5 minutes. Add orange rind, orange juice plus chicken broth and salt. Bring to a boil. Cover and cook over very low heat for about 18 to 22 minutes, until rice is tender and liquid is absorbed. Fluff with a fork and stir in slivered almonds and raisins.

HOT GARLIC GRILLED SHRIMP

Servings: 2-3

Shrimp grilled in the shell are juicy and have more flavor. This recipe is quite spicy, so cut back on the red pepper flakes if you wish. Allow the hot peppery garlic oil to cool before marinating the shrimp. Serve with **Sautéed Spinach**, *page 77.*

PEPPER OIL

½ cup vegetable oil
1 tbs. red pepper flakes
2 cloves finely minced garlic

1-1¼ lb. large shrimp in shells
1 fresh lime, cut into wedges

Place oil and red pepper flakes in a small heavy saucepan. Heat over low heat for 10 to 15 minutes until pepper flakes turn a light brown. Remove from heat, add minced garlic and allow to cool. When at room temperature, pour through a fine sieve. Discard garlic and pepper flakes.

Remove legs and cut shrimp shells down the back with a sharp pair of scissors. Pull out any vein, rinse and pat dry. Just before grilling, pour cooled pepper garlic oil over shrimp, spreading shells to allow oil to penetrate shrimp. Arrange on metal or presoaked wood skewers, pushing skewer through tail and top part of shrimp. Cook on a preheated grill for 3 to 4 minutes a side, until shells turn pink and shrimp are firm to the touch. Squeeze lime juice over cooked shrimp. Peel and eat.

SAUTÉED SPINACH

This aromatic spinach is tossed with pine nuts and raisins. It makes a delicious accompaniment for many grilled fish and chicken dishes.

2 bunches fresh spinach, about 12 oz. each, stemmed, washed
1 tbs. full-flavored olive oil
1 large clove garlic, minced
1 tbs. sherry wine vinegar
1 tbs. brown sugar
dash red pepper flakes
2 tbs. golden or dark raisins
salt and freshly ground pepper
1 tbs. lemon juice
¼ cup toasted pine nuts

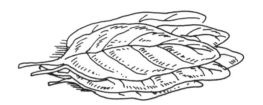

Blanch spinach in a large pot of boiling water for 30 to 45 seconds, drain and rinse with cold water. Squeeze dry. Combine olive oil, garlic, sherry vinegar, brown sugar, red pepper flakes and raisins in a medium skillet. Bring mixture to a boil, add spinach and cook for 1 to 2 minutes until spinach is hot. Season with salt, pepper and lemon juice. Pour into a serving dish, top with toasted pine nuts and serve.

SHRIMP WITH PESTO

Servings: 2-3 as a main dish

*Some supermarkets stock pesto in a tube, or in cartons in the refrigerator case or the freezer, which is acceptable if fresh basil is out of season, or you don't have time to make **Easy Pesto Sauce**, page 79. This is a great starter for a cookout. Serve as finger food with lots of napkins.*

1-1¼ lb. large shrimp in shells
2 tbs. prepared pesto
vegetable oil

Remove legs, cut shrimp shells down the back with a sharp pair of scissors, pull out vein, rinse and pat dry. Spread shell slightly and spoon about ¼ tsp. pesto into indentation where shrimp veins were removed, working pesto down between shell and shrimp. Thread shrimp on skewers, brush with oil and cook on a preheated grill for 3 to 4 minutes a side, until shells turn pink and shrimp are firm to the touch.

EASY PESTO SAUCE

Makes: ½ cup

This is delicious on grilled fish and chicken, or toss with some hot pasta.

1 cup lightly packed fresh basil leaves (about 1 oz.), or 1 small bunch
2 cloves garlic
⅓ cup toasted pine nuts, chopped almonds or walnuts
⅓ cup fruity olive oil
⅓ cup freshly grated Parmesan cheese
¼ tsp. salt, or to taste
freshly ground pepper

Place basil leaves, garlic, nuts and olive oil in a food processor bowl or blender container. Process until ingredients are well mixed, scraping down sides of container once or twice. Continue to process until mixture is fairly smooth. Pour into a bowl and stir in cheese, salt and pepper. This keeps well for 3 to 4 days in the refrigerator.

SHRIMP IN TEQUILA LIME MARINADE

Servings: 3-4

This easy marinade lets the wonderful shrimp flavors come through. Tabasco Jalapeño Sauce or another green jalapeño sauce adds a flavorful piquance.

¼ cup Tequila
grated rind (zest) from 1 lime
2 tbs. fresh lime juice
2 tbs. vegetable oil
1 tsp. Tabasco Jalapeño Sauce or other jalapeño sauce
1 lb. large shrimp (20-25 per lb.), peeled, deveined

Combine ingredients, except shrimp. Add prepared shrimp and marinate for 15 to 20 minutes, stirring occasionally. Thread shrimp on metal or presoaked wood skewers, keeping shrimp slightly curled so skewer goes through both tail and thicker part of body. Grill for 4 to 5 minutes a side until shrimp turn pink and are slightly firm to the touch.

TIGER SHRIMP WITH LEMON HONEY SAUCE

These shrimp can be grilled in their shells, or shelled and deveined prior to cooking, as you prefer. Choose large tiger shrimp, about 16 per pound.

1-1¼ lb. large tiger shrimp or other
  shrimp
vegetable oil for brushing
grated rind (zest) from 1 lemon

2 tbs. fresh lemon juice
2 tsp. honey
1 tbs. butter

Shell and devein shrimp. If grilling with shells, rinse shrimp, remove legs and cut down the back of the shrimp shells with sharp scissors. Open shell enough to devein shrimp with a sharp knife, keeping shrimp shell intact as much as possible. Arrange on metal or presoaked wood skewers. Cook on a preheated grill for about 3 to 4 minutes a side.

Using a lemon zester, remove zest from lemon in long strands. Combine zest, lemon juice, honey and butter in a small saucepan. Cook over low heat for about 5 minutes. Pour into small individual ramekins or a serving bowl. Peel and dip grilled shrimp in hot sauce.

GRILLED SHRIMP
WRAPPED IN PANCETTA

This is a terrific tasting and easy recipe. If you can't get pancetta, use very thinly sliced bacon. Serve with **Sautéed Spinach***, page 77.*

1 lb. large shrimp, peeled, deveined
3-4 tbs. hot sweet honey mustard
14-16 slices pancetta, or 8 slices bacon cut in half

Spread each shelled shrimp with about ½ tsp. honey mustard, coating both sides. If using bacon, blanch for 1 to 2 minutes in boiling water, or precook for 1 minute in the microwave. Wrap 1 slice pancetta or bacon half slice around each shrimp. Arrange shrimp on metal or presoaked wood skewers, pushing skewer through tail and top part of shrimp. Cook on a preheated grill for about 3 to 4 minutes a side, or until shrimp are firm to the touch.

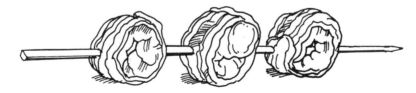

PEPPERED TUNA KABOBS

A blend of three different peppers provides a spicy to grilled fresh tuna. Use a spice grinder or peppermill to process the peppers into fairly small uniform pieces. Try this marinade on fresh salmon, too.

1 lb. fresh ahi tuna
¼ tsp. white peppercorns
¼ tsp. black peppercorns
¼ tsp. red pepper flakes, or to taste

¼ tsp. salt
1 tbs. lemon juice
1 tbs. olive oil

Cut tuna into 1½-inch chunks and thread on metal or presoaked wood skewers. Grind peppercorns, pepper flakes and salt together. Add mixture to lemon juice and olive oil. Brush tuna with pepper mixture and allow to marinate for 5 to 10 minutes. Cook on a preheated grill for about 2 minutes a side, turning once. Do not overcook.

GRILLED FRESH TUNA

Servings: 3-4

*Fresh ahi tuna is wonderful grilled and served with a simple soy and wasabi sauce. Buy sashimi-grade tuna that is safe to eat raw. Just sear the outside, leaving the middle rare. Buy the "wasabi," or horseradish powder, in the Asian or ethnic foods section of your supermarket. Serve with an **Orange Fennel Salad**, page 85.*

1 lb. fresh tuna
1 tsp. vegetable oil
2 tbs. soy sauce
1 tbs. rice wine vinegar
1/2 tsp. water
1 tsp. horseradish powder

Cut tuna in 1 1/2- to 2-inch chunks and thread on skewers. Brush with oil. Cook on a very hot preheated grill for about 2 minutes a side, turning once. Combine soy sauce and rice wine vinegar and pour into small individual sauce dishes for dipping. Mix water into horseradish powder and work into a paste. Place about 1/4 tsp. horseradish paste in each dish with soy and rice wine vinegar. Or, if desired, each person can stir wasabi into soy-vinegar sauce according to taste. Serve grilled tuna with dipping sauce.

ORANGE FENNEL SALAD

Servings: 3-4

This is a flavorful crisp salad to accompany grilled fish or chicken, or serve it as part of an antipasto platter. The feathery fennel greens can be finely chopped and sprinkled over the salad.

2-3 small fresh fennel bulbs
2 medium oranges
1 small red onion, peeled, thinly sliced
2 tbs. olive oil
1 tbs. sherry wine vinegar

1/4 tsp. ground cumin
salt and freshly ground pepper
small black olives or finely chopped
  fennel greens for garnish

Cut straight across rounded top of fennel bulb, removing feathery greens and other growth. Remove tough outer layer of bulb and slice vertically into thin slices with a knife or the slicing blade of a food processor. Place slices in a shallow serving bowl. Remove orange peel and white membrane with a sharp knife, cutting from top to bottom of orange. Remove orange segments by cutting down each side of the membrane that separates the segments, and place in bowl with fennel. Add onion slices. Squeeze remaining orange juice from oranges into a small bowl; add olive oil, sherry wine vinegar, cumin, salt and pepper. Mix well and toss with fennel and oranges. Garnish with small black olives, or sprinkle with finely chopped fennel greens.

GRILLED TUNA SALAD NIÇOISE

Servings: 2-3

Wonderful fresh tuna and new potatoes are grilled and then sauced with a lemon anchovy dressing. The recipe can be doubled easily if needed. If you have fresh thyme or rosemary, brush small pieces with oil and tuck sprigs between the tuna chunks before grilling. This is also delicious made with grilled fresh salmon.

1 lb. new potatoes
1 lb. green beans, stemmed
1 tbs. full-flavored olive oil
1 tbs. lemon juice
1 tsp. fresh thyme leaves
salt and freshly ground pepper
1 lb. fresh tuna, cut into 1½-inch chunks
sprigs fresh thyme or rosemary
fresh mixed salad greens, or romaine or escarole
Dressing, follows
2 large ripe tomatoes, peeled, seeded, cut into wedges
2 hard-cooked eggs, cut into wedges, optional
6-8 roasted red bell pepper strips, or crisp red or green bell pepper rings
black niçoise or kalamata olives
1-2 tbs. rinsed, drained capers

Cook unpeeled new potatoes until just tender. Drain and let cool for a few minutes. Cook green beans until tender.

Combine olive oil, lemon juice, thyme leaves, salt and pepper. Brush oil and herb mixture on tuna pieces and roll cooked new potatoes in remaining mixture. Thread tuna on oiled skewers, alternating with potatoes, or make separate skewers for tuna and potatoes. Grill tuna for about 4 to 6 minutes a side, or until slightly firm to the touch.

To assemble: Toss salad greens with 1 to 2 tbs. dressing. Spoon a little dressing over cooked green beans and toss. Arrange individual plates with some dressed salad greens. Top with green beans, tomato wedges, egg wedges, red pepper strips and olives. Sprinkle with capers. Divide grilled new potatoes and tuna between plates and spoon some dressing over both. Pass remaining dressing in a small bowl for potatoes.

DRESSING

1/4 cup full-flavored olive oil
1 tbs. lemon juice
1 tbs. Dijon mustard
1 tbs. white wine vinegar

1/2 tsp. sugar
1 tsp. anchovy paste
salt and freshly ground pepper

In a small bowl, whip ingredients together until mixture combines smoothly.

GRILLED SALMON AND MUSHROOM KABOBS

Grilled salmon and mushrooms make a terrific combination when accented with **Sun-Dried Tomato Relish**, *and served on some creamy* **Easy Polenta**, *page 89. The salmon just needs a very light coat of oil or cooking spray before grilling.*

1 lb. medium-sized brown cremini mushrooms
olive oil or sun-dried tomato oil for brushing
1 lb. salmon steaks, skinned, boned, cut into 1-inch cubes

Remove stems from mushrooms and clean. Brush mushrooms with a little olive oil, or some of the sun-dried tomato oil. Arrange salmon pieces alternately with mushrooms on metal or presoaked wood skewers. Cook on a preheated grill for about 6 to 8 minutes a side, or until salmon is firm to the touch and lightly browned.

SUN-DRIED TOMATO RELISH
½ cup chopped oil-packed sun-dried tomatoes
1 tbs. balsamic vinegar
salt and freshly ground pepper

Combine tomatoes, vinegar and seasonings. Spoon over grilled salmon, mushrooms and polenta.

EASY POLENTA

*Polenta cooks beautifully in the microwave with just a couple of quick stirs. Use your favorite cheeses and imagination for variations on this side dish. Some leftover **Sauce Vera Cruz**, page 95, is wonderful spooned over it.*

½ cup polenta cornmeal
2½ cups water
½ tsp. salt
1 tbs. butter, softened
2 oz. Italian fontina or Gorgonzola cheese, cut into small cubes

Use a deep microwavable dish that will be less than half full with the cornmeal water mixture, because it will bubble up during cooking.

Combine polenta cornmeal, water and salt in microwavable dish, stirring to combine. Cook, uncovered, on high for 5 to 6 minutes. Remove from oven, stir, cover with a paper towel and return to microwave. Cook for another 5 to 6 minutes. Most of the liquid should have been absorbed by the cornmeal. If mixture is too watery, cook for another minute. Stir in softened butter and cheese. Covered, this will keep warm for several minutes until you are ready to serve. It can be reheated in the microwave.

SALMON PINWHEELS

Do these for a special dinner party. They marinate quickly and are easy to eat. Serve with garlic mashed potatoes, fresh asparagus and a crisp Chardonnay.

4 salmon steaks, about ¾-inch thick,
  about 8 oz. each
olive oil
salt and freshly ground pepper
2 tbs. lemon juice

1 tbs. butter, melted
1 tbs. lemon juice
¼ tsp. dried tarragon, or 1 tsp. finely
  chopped fresh
salt and freshly ground pepper

Remove skin and carefully cut down along the center bone, freeing salmon strips. Wrap the thin tail around the wider part to form a circular pinwheel. Push a metal or presoaked wood skewer through the middle of each pinwheel to keep it from unwinding. Brush both sides of pinwheels with olive oil, salt and pepper and sprinkle generously with lemon juice. Marinate for about 10 minutes. When grill is hot, cook for 4 to 5 minutes a side until fish is firm to the touch. Do not overcook. Combine melted butter, lemon juice, tarragon, salt and pepper. Remove pinwheels from skewers, place on serving plates and pour butter sauce over fish. Serve immediately.

GINGER- AND SOY-GLAZED SALMON KABOBS

This quick marinade produces succulent, brown pieces of salmon. Serve on a bed of thinly sliced cucumbers dressed with a little rice wine vinegar and a pinch of sugar, or on some lightly dressed arugula leaves.

1 lb. salmon steaks
1 tbs. vegetable oil
2 tbs. soy sauce
1 tsp. brown sugar
1 tsp. finely minced or grated ginger root
$\frac{1}{4}$ tsp. sesame oil
6 green onions, white part only, cut into 1-inch pieces, optional

Remove skin and bone from salmon steaks and cut into 1-inch cubes. Combine oil, soy sauce, sugar, ginger and sesame oil. Toss salmon cubes with marinade. Arrange salmon pieces on metal or presoaked wood skewers, alternating salmon with pieces of green onion. Cook on a preheated grill for about 6 to 8 minutes a side, or until salmon is firm to the touch and lightly browned. Brush once or twice with marinade during grilling.

GRILLED SEAFOOD SKEWER MEALS 91

GRILLED SALMON
WITH CREAMY CABBAGE

Salmon chunks are simply grilled and served on a bed of wine-flavored cabbage. This makes a terrific appetizer course for 4, accompanied by a crisp Chardonnay.

1 lb. fresh salmon, cut into 1¼-inch cubes
vegetable oil
salt and pepper
5 tbs. butter
6 cups shredded napa or savoy
  cabbage, about 1 lb.
1 small shallot, finely chopped
1 tbs. sherry wine vinegar
¼ cup white wine or dry vermouth
minced fresh parsley for garnish

Arrange salmon pieces on metal or presoaked wood skewers; brush with oil, salt and pepper. Cook on a preheated grill for about 6 to 8 minutes a side, or until lightly browned and slightly firm to the touch. In a large skillet, melt 2 tbs. of the butter and sauté cabbage for 2 to 3 minutes over medium heat until cabbage softens. Stir frequently, making sure cabbage doesn't brown. Combine shallots, sherry wine vinegar and white wine in a small saucepan; bring to a boil. Cook until liquid reduces to about half. Gradually stir in remaining 3 tbs. butter over low heat until sauce thickens slightly. Pour sauce over cabbage and heat to blend flavors. Taste and adjust seasoning if necessary. Place some cabbage in the center of each serving plate, top with grilled salmon, sprinkle with parsley and serve immediately.

RED SNAPPER KABOBS
WITH SAUCE VERA CRUZ

Servings: 3-4

*This features a piquant Mexican-style sauce with tomatoes, olives, capers and onions. Serve with some hot cooked pasta or rice, or **Easy Polenta**, page 89.*

1½ lb. red snapper or other firm-fleshed fish, skinned, boned
1 tbs. olive oil mixed with 1 tbs. lime juice

SAUCE VERA CRUZ
2 tbs. olive oil
½ cup chopped onion
2 cloves garlic, minced
1 can (15½ oz.) tomato pieces, drained
2-3 tsp. chopped pickled jalapeño pepper or jalapeño "nacho slices"
½ tsp. dried marjoram
½ tsp. dried thyme
pinch cinnamon
⅓ cup sliced pimiento-stuffed green olives
1 tbs. rinsed, drained capers
salt and freshly ground pepper
2-3 tbs. coarsely chopped fresh cilantro leaves

Cut fish into 1½-inch pieces and thread on metal or presoaked wood skewers. Brush with oil and lime juice. Grill for about 6 to 8 minutes a side, until firm.

Heat 2 tbs. olive oil in a medium saucepan and sauté onion for 5 to 6 minutes until softened. Add garlic, cook for 1 minute, and stir in tomatoes, jalapeño, marjoram, thyme and cinnamon. Bring to a boil and cook for 5 minutes. Add olives and capers. Season with salt and pepper and cook for 1 to 2 more minutes. Stir in cilantro and spoon over grilled fish.

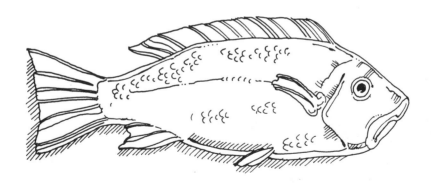

GRILLED FISH KABOBS
WITH LEMON CAPER SAUCE

Use firm-fleshed fish such as halibut, red snapper or swordfish for easier grilling. Serve with some hot cooked rice to soak up the delicious sauce.

1½ lb. firm-fleshed fish, skinned, boned, cut into 1½-inch pieces
1 tbs. oil mixed with 1 tbs. lemon juice

LEMON CAPER SAUCE

⅓ cup white wine
⅓ cup chicken stock
2 tbs. lemon juice
2 tbs. butter

3 tbs. rinsed, drained capers
salt and freshly ground pepper
1 tbs. finely chopped fresh parsley

Arrange fish on metal or presoaked wood skewers. Brush fish with oil-lemon juice mixture. Cook on a preheated grill for about 6 to 8 minutes a side, or until fish is firm to the touch and lightly browned. While fish is grilling, combine wine, chicken stock and lemon juice in a small saucepan. Bring to a boil and reduce to ⅓ cup. Stir in butter and capers. Season with salt and pepper, and stir in parsley. Pass a small bowl of sauce to spoon over fish.

HALIBUT KABOBS
WITH THAI BASIL SAUCE

Creamy coconut milk is the base for this quick sauce. Fish sauce adds a unique flavor and can be found in the Asian food section of most supermarkets. Steamed fragrant jasmine rice and crisp green broccoli would be delicious accompaniments.

1 lb. halibut or other firm-fleshed fish, boned, trimmed
1 tbs. olive oil mixed with 1 tbs. lime juice
1 cup canned coconut milk
1 tsp. finely grated ginger root
2 tbs. fish sauce
grated rind (zest) from 1 lime
2 tbs. fresh lime juice
1/2 tsp. Tabasco Jalapeño Sauce
pinch white pepper
1 tsp. cornstarch dissolved in 1 tbs. water
2 small green onions, finely sliced
10-12 fresh basil leaves, rolled and cut into ribbons

Cut fish into 1½-inch cubes. Thread on metal or presoaked wood skewers; brush with oil-lime juice mixture. Cook on a preheated grill for about 6 to 8 minutes a side, or until slightly firm to the touch and lightly browned. Combine coconut milk, ginger, fish sauce, lime zest and juice, Tabasco and white pepper. Bring to a boil and cook for 5 minutes, stirring occasionally. Just before serving, stir in dissolved cornstarch, bring to a boil and cook for 2 to 3 minutes to thicken. Garnish with green onions and basil ribbons and serve.

GRILLED CALAMARI SALAD

Quick grilling keeps calamari very tender. You will need about 1 lb. squid to yield ½ lb. cleaned squid. Serve this Mexican-style salad with hot garlic bread.

½ lb. cleaned squid, about 3-4 large
  squid
olive oil for brushing
2 red ripe tomatoes, peeled, seeded,
  chopped
2 green onions, white part only, thinly
  sliced
¼ tsp. dried oregano

2 tsp. rinsed, drained capers
2 tbs. full-flavored olive oil
1 tsp. lemon juice
2 tsp. balsamic vinegar
salt and freshly ground pepper
2 tbs. chopped fresh parsley
butter lettuce leaves or mixed greens

Cut squid bodies open to form one flat piece. Thread two presoaked wood skewers about 1 to 2 inches apart vertically through squid, or thread one skewer vertically and one horizontally. Spray or brush with a little olive oil. Cook on a preheated grill for about 1½ minutes a side, just until grill marks appear and squid turns opaque. *Do not overcook.* Remove from skewers and slice into strips. Combine tomatoes, onions, oregano and capers in a small bowl with squid strips. Whisk together 2 tbs. olive oil, lemon juice, balsamic vinegar, salt, pepper and parsley; pour over salad and toss. Spoon mixture into butter lettuce cups or over mixed greens and serve.

GRILLED BEEF, PORK AND LAMB SKEWER MEALS

What smells better than steak, hamburger or marinated lamb grilling over a fire? Meat is still the main event for many parties, but smaller quantities are being consumed in keeping with today's healthy eating trends. Kabobs are a great way to satisfy the need for a protein fix. Skewer a vegetable or two with the meat, and make serving a snap.

Lamb and grilling go together, and included are a variety of marinades. Try *Lamb Chops with Pomegranate Juice* for a special dinner for two, or *Grilled Lamb with Hoisin Orange Glaze*. Middle Eastern flavors of *Yogurt-Marinated Lamb Kabobs*, or savory ground lamb sausages, are paired with a flavorful *Greek Salad* or *Tabbouleh*. Herbes de Provence make a simple marinade for *Provençal Lamb Kabobs* and grilled vegetables.

If beef is your pleasure, try *Mahogany Steak Kabobs* or flavorful *Oyster Sauce Steak Chunks*. If you like it spicy, make *Grilled Flank Steak with Chipotle Chile Marinade*. Pork, the other white meat, takes a fruity apple marinade in *Apple-Glazed Pork Strips*. Other delicious recipes are *Marmalade-Glazed Pork Skewers* with a *Creamy Potato Gratin*, and *Pork Carnitas-Style* that is served with warm tortillas and all the trimmings.

We've also included a great grilled liver and bacon with slow cooked *Cabernet Onions* and *Grilled Sausages* to serve with *Lentil Salad* or *Black Bean and Salsa Salad*. There are quick recipes for grilled ham and fruit kabobs, too.

SOUVLAKIA

This Greek classic is one of the simplest and also one of the best kabob recipes. Double the marinade if you are using a small leg of lamb and cooking for 4 to 6 people. Serve this with **Green Chile and Rice Bake**, *page 103.*

MARINADE

1 large onion
2 tbs. olive oil
1 tbs. lemon juice

1 tsp. chopped garlic
½ tsp. dried oregano
freshly ground pepper

1 lb. lamb leg pieces, trimmed of all fat, cut into 2-inch cubes
½ red bell pepper, cored, cut into 1½-inch squares

Remove large outer onion leaves and reserve. Slice remaining onion into ½-inch slices. Combine onion and remaining marinade ingredients in a plastic bag. Add lamb cubes, close bag, removing as much air as possible, and marinate for at least 4 hours or overnight in the refrigerator. Turn bag occasionally to assure even marinating. Cut reserved onion leaves into 1½-inch square pieces. Remove lamb from the refrigerator about 1 hour before cooking. Arrange drained meat on metal or presoaked wood skewers, alternating meat with red pepper and onion pieces. Grill over a hot fire for about 10 to 12 minutes a side, turning once. Serve immediately.

GREEN CHILE AND RICE BAKE

Servings: 2-3

This can be done ahead and reheated in the oven or microwave just before serving. Roasted, peeled fresh pasilla peppers make a delicious substitute for the canned green chiles.

2¾ cups water
1½ cups uncooked long-grain rice
salt
⅓ cup chopped canned chiles or
  roasted, peeled green chiles
¼ cup chopped roasted red bell
  peppers or pimiento
½ cup grated Monterey Jack cheese

½ cup grated sharp cheddar cheese
1 tsp. Tabasco Jalapeño Sauce
salt and freshly ground pepper
½ cup coarsely chopped fresh cilantro
  leaves
1½-2 cups sour cream
additional cilantro leaves for garnish

Bring water to a boil in a large saucepan; add rice and salt. Cover, lower heat and simmer for 18 to 20 minutes until rice is cooked and tender. Combine remaining ingredients, except sour cream and whole cilantro leaves, and stir into cooked rice. Add enough sour cream to make rice mixture creamy. It should be quite moist. Spoon rice into an ovenproof casserole. Cover casserole and place in a preheated 350° oven for 25 to 30 minutes until hot. Sprinkle with fresh cilantro leaves before serving.

YOGURT-MARINATED LAMB KABOBS

*Yogurt is a great meat tenderizer and requires a short marinating time. If you can, drain the yogurt in a sieve in the refrigerator for 2 to 3 hours, or overnight, to get rid of the excess moisture. Serve with **Tabbouleh**, page 105, and melon slices.*

MARINADE

1/4 cup chopped onion
2 cloves garlic, peeled
1/2 jalapeño pepper, stemmed, seeded
1/4 cup loosely packed fresh mint leaves
1 cup drained plain yogurt
1 tbs. olive oil
1/2 tsp. ground ginger

1/4 tsp. ground cumin
1/4 tsp. ground coriander
1/4 tsp. dry mustard
pinch cinnamon
pinch ground cloves
pinch mace
salt and freshly ground pepper

2 lb. leg of lamb, trimmed of all fat, cut into 1 1/2-inch cubes

Combine onion, garlic, jalapeño and mint leaves in a food processor bowl and process until finely chopped. Add remaining marinade ingredients and pulse to blend. Pour over lamb cubes, toss to coat, and marinate for about 1 hour at cool room temperature. Thread lamb cubes on metal or presoaked wood skewers and cook for 8 to 10 minutes a side on a preheated grill.

TABBOULEH

This Middle Eastern salad made with bulghur, parsley and tomatoes goes beautifully with many grilled dishes. Spoon it into crisp romaine leaves and serve on a large platter. Make this 2 to 3 hours before serving and let it stand in a cool place. This also makes a great filling for hollowed-out ripe tomatoes for a buffet.

1 cup bulghur
2 cups boiling water
1 cup finely chopped peeled, seeded
  tomatoes
1/2 cup finely chopped fresh parsley,
  about 2 cups loosely packed leaves
2 tbs. minced green onions

2 tbs. finely chopped fresh mint leaves
3 tbs. lemon juice
1 tbs. olive oil
salt and freshly ground pepper
romaine lettuce leaves
toasted sesame seeds and whole mint
  leaves for garnish

Place bulghur in a small bowl, cover with boiling water and let stand for about 30 minutes, or follow package directions, until grains are tender. Drain and squeeze very dry. Place in a medium bowl and add tomatoes, parsley, green onions, chopped mint leaves, lemon juice, olive oil, salt and pepper. Toss to combine. Just before serving, spoon into lettuce leaves and sprinkle with sesame seeds and a few mint leaves.

LAMB CHOPS WITH POMEGRANATE JUICE

Servings: 2

*Try this recipe when you want a special dinner for two. Small loin lamb chops are marinated in fresh pomegranate juice and onions, and then grilled. This is good with chunks of boneless leg of lamb, too. Serve with **Tuscan-Style Beans**, page 63, and a crisp green salad. Use an orange or lemon juicer to remove juice from pomegranates. Pomegranate juice also can be found in Middle Eastern markets or health food stores.*

4 small loin lamb chops, about 1-inch thick, well trimmed
1 small onion, thinly sliced
1/3 cup fresh pomegranate juice, about 3-4 small pomegranates
freshly ground pepper

Place trimmed lamb chops in a plastic bag or small glass or stainless steel pan. Top with sliced onion, pomegranate juice and a generous amount of pepper. Marinate for 30 to 40 minutes, turning occasionally. Using metal or presoaked wood skewers, run skewer diagonally through meaty part of chops. Cook on a preheated grill for about 6 to 8 minutes a side, turning once.

GRILLED LAMB WITH HOISIN ORANGE GLAZE

*This full-bodied marinade is delicious with lamb or beef. Hoisin and oyster sauces can usually be found in the supermarket in the Asian or ethnic food section. Marinate for 3 to 4 hours or overnight in the refrigerator before grilling. Serve with **Creamy Potato Gratin**, page 127, and crisp broccoli or asparagus.*

2 lb. boneless leg of lamb
3 tbs. undiluted frozen orange juice
  concentrate
2 tbs. oyster sauce

1 tbs. red wine vinegar
2 tbs. hoisin sauce
1 tbs. vegetable oil
dash red pepper flakes

Trim lamb, removing all fat and gristle, and cut into 1½- to 2-inch square chunks. Combine remaining ingredients. Place lamb in a plastic bag or stainless steel or glass bowl and pour marinade over lamb, mixing well. Marinate in the refrigerator for at least 3 to 4 hours, and remove about 30 minutes before grilling. Arrange marinated lamb on metal or presoaked wood skewers and cook on a preheated grill over high heat for about 13 to 15 minutes until lamb is slightly springy to the touch, about 140° on an instant-read thermometer. Turn once or twice during grilling. Serve hot.

GRILLED CURRIED LAMB KABOBS

Servings: 3-4

*Serve this aromatic lamb with **Herbed Pilaf**, page 43, a fresh fruit salad and some sliced cucumbers dressed with yogurt and a little mint or dill.*

MARINADE

2 tbs. vegetable oil
½ tsp. curry powder
1 tsp. grated ginger root
½ tsp. ground cumin
½ tsp. dry mustard

¼ tsp. cinnamon
pinch ground cloves
2 large cloves garlic, minced
2 tbs. soy sauce
freshly ground pepper

2 lb. leg of lamb, trimmed of all fat, cut into 1½-inch cubes

In small skillet, gently heat vegetable oil with curry powder for 1 to 2 minutes to release curry flavor. Combine with remaining marinade ingredients in a bowl and toss with lamb chunks until well mixed. Cover and refrigerate for 3 to 4 hours or overnight. Remove from refrigerator about 30 minutes before grilling. Thread lamb on metal or presoaked wood skewers and cook on a preheated grill for about 8 to 10 minutes a side.

PROVENÇAL LAMB KABOBS

Herbes de Provence give a wonderful South-of-France flavor to this savory marinade. This herb blend includes basil, fennel, lavender, rosemary, thyme, marjoram and sage, and is usually found in small ceramic pots in the spice section of the supermarket. Serve with roasted red and yellow peppers garnished with tiny black olives, and **Creamy Potato Gratin***, page 127.*

1/4 cup full-flavored olive oil
2 tsp. dried herbes de Provence
1 large clove garlic, finely minced
2 tbs. red wine vinegar
salt and freshly ground pepper
2 lb. leg of lamb, trimmed of all fat, cut into 2-inch cubes

Combine olive oil, herbs, garlic, vinegar, salt and pepper. Toss lamb cubes with oil mixture, cover and refrigerate for 3 to 4 hours or overnight. Thread lamb on metal or presoaked wood skewers and cook on a preheated grill for about 10 to 12 minutes a side.

HERBED LAMB KABOBS

Servings: 3-4

*Fresh herbs and pepper are pressed into the meat to make a savory flavorful crust when grilled. Serve with oven-roasted potato wedges, **Provençal Vegetables**, page 111, and a full-bodied red wine. Soak whole bay leaves in water for 20 minutes, cut in half and skewer between meat cubes.*

2 lb. leg of lamb, trimmed of all fat, cut into 2-inch cubes
3 tbs. full-flavored olive oil
10-12 bay leaves, optional
1/4 cup fresh thyme or finely chopped oregano leaves
3 tbs. finely minced shallot
1/2 tsp. salt
freshly ground pepper
2 tsp. balsamic vinegar

Generously brush lamb cubes with olive oil and thread on metal or presoaked wood skewers with bay leaves. Combine thyme leaves, shallot and salt. Firmly press mixture into lamb cubes. Coarsely grind a generous amount of pepper over lamb and press into meat. Cook on a preheated grill for about 8 to 10 minutes a side. Remove from heat, sprinkle with balsamic vinegar and serve immediately.

PROVENÇAL VEGETABLES

Servings: 4-6

A vegetable melange of eggplant, ripe tomatoes, squash, onions and garlic bake together. Make this a day or two ahead if you like. It can be served hot, warm or at room temperature. If you have some left over, toss with hot cooked pasta and a little more Parmesan cheese to make a quick lunch or supper.

2-3 Japanese eggplants, cut into large dice
4 small zucchini or yellow squash, or some of each, cut into large dice
2 red, yellow or green bell peppers, cored, seeded, cut into large dice
1½ cups coarsely chopped onions
1 generous cup coarsely chopped, seeded tomatoes
2 tbs. full-flavored olive oil

3 cloves garlic, finely chopped
½ tsp. dried oregano or 1 tbs. fresh
1 tsp. dried thyme, or 1 tbs. fresh
1 tsp. dried basil, or 2 tbs. minced fresh
dash red pepper flakes
salt and freshly ground pepper
⅓ cup dry white or red wine
⅓ cup grated Parmesan cheese

Preheat oven to 375°. Place vegetables in a medium ovenproof casserole with a lid. Toss vegetables with oil, garlic, herbs, red pepper flakes, salt and pepper. Pour in wine, cover and bake for 1 hour. Remove cover and bake for 20 minutes or until vegetables are tender and most of liquid has evaporated. Top with Parmesan cheese before serving.

GRILLED KEFTEDES

Servings: 3-4

*These Greek-style ground lamb sausages make a terrific pita filling, or serve them with a **Greek Salad**, page 113, or **Tabbouleh**, page 105. Chilling the formed keftedes in the refrigerator for at least 1 hour makes them stay on the skewers for easier grilling. A metal spatula is helpful in turning the keftedes on the grill.*

1 lb. lean ground lamb
1 egg white
1 tsp. Pernod, or anise-flavored liqueur
2 tbs. minced fresh Italian parsley
2 tsp. dried dill weed
1 large clove garlic, finely chopped

1 tbs. lemon juice
1 tbs. olive oil
1 tsp. salt
1/4 tsp. freshly ground pepper
3 tbs. cracker crumbs

Combine ingredients in a medium bowl, mixing well with hands. Divide into 12 equal pieces. Form each piece into a sausage shape about 1 inch in diameter and 2 inches long. Thread 3 keftedes on each of four 12-inch-long flat metal skewers. Refrigerate for at least 1 hour to firm. Cook on a preheated grill for about 8 to 10 minutes, turning once, until crusty on outside, but still juicy.

GREEK SALAD

Crisp lettuce, cucumbers, tomatoes and olives are tossed with some feta cheese for a terrific accompaniment to grilled meats, chicken or fish.

1 small head iceberg lettuce, torn into
  bite-sized pieces
1 medium cucumber, peeled, seeded,
  thinly sliced
1 small red onion, thinly sliced
1 red or yellow bell pepper, peeled,
  seeded, thinly sliced
2 medium ripe tomatoes, peeled,
  seeded, cut into thin wedges

8-10 fresh mint leaves, finely minced
4 oz. feta cheese, coarsely crumbled
10-12 kalamata olives
1 tbs. drained, rinsed capers
salt and freshly ground pepper
Dressing, follows

Combine salad ingredients in a large serving bowl. Toss with dressing.

DRESSING

⅓ cup full-flavored olive oil
1 tbs. fresh oregano leaves, or 1 tsp. dried
1 clove garlic

1 tbs. red wine vinegar
1 tbs. lemon juice
salt and freshly ground pepper

Combine ingredients in blender container and process until smooth.

KIBBE KABOBS

Bulghur and ground lamb meatballs are served in pita pockets and topped with a sauce of goat cheese and roasted garlic. Start soaking the bulghur an hour or so before you are ready to assemble the kibbe, and allow time to chill before grilling. Roast the garlic while the kabobs are chilling.

½ cup bulghur
1 cup boiling water
½ lb. lean ground lamb or turkey
2 tbs. diced onion
1 tbs. olive oil
½ tsp. salt
¼ tsp. ground cumin

½ tsp. paprika
2 tsp. cornstarch
1 tbs. chopped fresh mint, or 1 tsp. dried
Goat Cheese and Roasted Garlic Sauce,
 page 115

Place bulghur in a small bowl and pour in boiling water. Allow to stand for 30 to 45 minutes; drain well in a sieve. Add all ingredients, including bulghur, to a food processor bowl. Process until mixture forms a smooth paste. Form mixture into 12 to 16 equal balls. Thread on 4 flat-sided metal skewers and refrigerate for at least 1 hour to firm. Grill over a hot fire until brown, turning frequently, about 12 to 14 minutes. Serve in warm pita breads and top with *Goat Cheese and Roasted Garlic Sauce.*

GOAT CHEESE AND
ROASTED GARLIC SAUCE

This sauce makes a delicious topping for baked potatoes, or thin it with a little milk and use it as a dip for grilled vegetables. Do 2 or 3 heads of garlic at the same time and refrigerate the extras for making garlic bread or garlic mashed potatoes.

1 head garlic, unpeeled
1 tsp. olive oil
4 oz. creamy fresh goat cheese
1/3-1/2 cup milk
2 tbs. finely minced fresh parsley
salt and freshly ground pepper

Preheat oven to 375°. Cut about 1/2 inch from top of garlic head. Place garlic on a piece of kitchen foil. Drizzle cut surfaces of garlic with olive oil and fold up foil tightly around garlic. Place garlic on a small metal pie plate or pan and roast in oven for about 45 minutes. Check with tip of a knife to make sure cloves are soft; unwrap garlic.

Mash 3 cloves roasted garlic with a fork and stir into crumbled goat cheese. Thin with a few drops of milk until mixture is smooth and thin enough to pour. Stir in parsley, salt and pepper.

MAHOGANY STEAK KABOBS

Servings: 4

A little molasses and a few drops of Liquid Smoke give a marvelous flavor and color to these juicy hunks of steak. Use top sirloin, New York strip or Delmonico steaks. Serve these with baked potatoes with **Goat Cheese and Roasted Garlic Sauce**, *page 115, and* **Black Bean and Salsa Salad**, *page 117.*

1½ lb. boneless steak, cut into 1¼-inch cubes
vegetable oil for brushing
2 tbs. chicken stock
2 tbs. molasses
1 tbs. sherry wine vinegar
½ tsp. Tabasco Jalapeño Sauce
¼ tsp. Liquid Smoke
salt and freshly ground pepper

With meat at room temperature, thread steak cubes on metal or presoaked wood skewers. Brush with vegetable oil. Combine remaining ingredients in a small saucepan and heat. Cook steak skewers on a preheated grill over high heat for about 3 to 4 minutes a side. Brush with molasses mixture 2 to 3 times during grilling.

BLACK BEAN AND SALSA SALAD

Servings: 3-4

Here is a colorful zesty salad to accompany grilled steaks, chicken or fish. Use your favorite fresh salsa and garnish with fresh cilantro leaves just before serving. This recipe is easily doubled.

1 can (15 oz.) black beans
½ cup fresh salsa, hot or mild
1 small ripe avocado, peeled, diced, optional
fresh cilantro leaves for garnish

Drain beans, rinse with cold water and drain well. Pour beans into a serving bowl, add salsa and refrigerate until ready to serve. Just before serving, stir in avocado and top with cilantro leaves.

THAI-STYLE GRILLED STEAK SATAYS

Servings: 2-3

A spicy peanut sauce tops these delicious grilled steak strips. Serve with steamed rice and a fruit salad. Find hot chile paste with garlic where Asian foods are sold.

1 lb. flank steak, trimmed of all fat
2 tbs. vegetable oil
1 tbs. lime juice

1 clove garlic, minced
fresh cilantro leaves for garnish

PEANUT SAUCE
1/2 cup chicken stock
1/3 cup creamy peanut butter
1 tbs. minced ginger root
1 tbs. lime juice
1 tbs. soy sauce

1 tsp. brown sugar
1/2 tsp. hot chile paste with garlic, or 1 clove garlic, finely chopped and 1/4 tsp. red pepper flakes

With knife at a 45-degree angle, cut flank steak into 1/8-inch-thin diagonal slices across the grain. Thread steak strips on metal or presoaked wood skewers. Combine oil, lime juice and garlic. Brush mixture on steak strips and marinate for about 30 minutes. Combine peanut sauce ingredients in a small saucepan and bring to a boil. Remove from heat. Cook steak strips on a preheated grill for about 3 to 4 minutes a side. Serve warm sauce in a small bowl in the middle of the table for dipping. Garnish plates with fresh cilantro leaves.

BEEF AND MUSHROOM TERIYAKI

The less expensive fillet tails work well in this recipe. Use flavorful Italian brown cremini mushrooms, if you can find them. Serve with crisp green broccoli or asparagus, and cooked pasta tossed with butter, parsley and Parmesan cheese.

1 lb. beef fillet or fillet tails
10-12 medium fresh mushrooms (1½-inch diameter)
6 green onions, trimmed, cut into 2-inch lengths

MARINADE
¼ cup soy sauce
⅓ cup dry sherry or Shaoxing rice wine
1 tbs. finely minced ginger root

1 tsp. sesame oil
1 tbs. red wine vinegar

Cut beef into 8 cubes, about 1 inch on each side. If using fillet tails, cut into 1-inch-wide strips and roll up into 1-inch pieces. Remove stems from mushrooms. Combine marinade ingredients in a small bowl or a plastic bag. Add meat, mushrooms and onions, and marinate for at least 20 minutes before grilling. Remove from marinade, drain and thread on metal or presoaked wood skewers, alternating meat, mushrooms and onions. Grill over very high heat for 8 to 10 minutes, turning once. Brush with marinade while cooking.

SAUERBRATEN KABOBS

Servings: 4

*This German-style dish has a wonderful ginger-spiced sauce. **Potato Pancakes**, page 121, and applesauce are perfect accompaniments.*

MARINADE

1 cup red wine
1 cup vegetable broth
1 small onion, peeled, thinly sliced
3 tbs. lemon juice

1 tbs. sugar
1/2 tsp. allspice
4 whole cloves

1 1/2 lb. boneless steak, trimmed, cut
  into 1 1/2-inch chunks
1 tbs. tomato paste

3-4 gingersnaps, crushed
salt and freshly ground pepper

Heat marinade ingredients in a small saucepan to boiling. Remove from heat and cool to room temperature. Add to beef cubes and marinate at a cool room temperature for about 4 hours or overnight in the refrigerator. Remove beef from marinade and thread on metal or presoaked wood skewers. Strain marinade into a small saucepan and bring to a boil. Cook over high heat until reduced to about 1 cup. Add tomato paste and gingersnap crumbs; cook until sauce thickens. Season with salt and pepper. Cook meat on a preheated grill for about 6 to 8 minutes a side. Serve with hot sauce.

POTATO PANCAKES

These great crispy potatoes can be done before you start grilling the meat and kept warm for 15 to 20 minutes in a 250° oven. Use a food processor to grate the potatoes.

1 lb. baking potatoes
1 egg, beaten
1 tbs. mayonnaise
1 tbs. flour

salt and white pepper
2 green onions, finely sliced, optional
vegetable oil for frying

Peel and coarsely grate potatoes just before cooking. Place grated potatoes on several layers of paper towels and blot well to remove excess moisture. Combine potatoes with remaining ingredients in a bowl and mix well. Heat a large nonstick skillet with vegetable oil to a depth of about $1/8$ inch. When oil is hot, add heaping spoonfuls of potato mixture, spread and flatten a little with a spatula. Cook over medium heat for about 4 to 5 minutes a side, or until brown and cooked through. Drain on paper towels and serve immediately, or place on a plate with paper towels and keep warm in the oven for 15 to 20 minutes.

OYSTER SAUCE STEAK CHUNKS

Servings: 4

Chinese oyster sauce adds a rich taste note to the marinade for these juicy steak kabobs. Use your favorite steak: fillet, top sirloin, New York strip or Delmonico. **Grilled Onion Wedges**, *page 153, fresh asparagus and* **Oven-Roasted Potato Wedges**, *page 123, are delicious accompaniments.*

MARINADE
2 tbs. oyster sauce
2 tbs. dry sherry or Shaoxing wine
1 tbs. light soy sauce
salt
finely ground white pepper
1 tsp. sesame oil
1 tbs. vegetable oil

1½ lb. boneless steak, cut into 1¼-inch cubes

Mix marinade ingredients together. Toss steak cubes in marinade and allow to marinate for 30 minutes at room temperature. Arrange meat on metal or presoaked wood skewers and grill over high heat for 3 to 4 minutes a side, or until cooked to your preference.

OVEN-ROASTED POTATO WEDGES

Servings: 4

These simple crisp potato wedges are addictive. They are healthful — as good as French fries, but with much less fat. Add a few dried or fresh herbs or a pinch of cumin or chili powder to the olive oil for a variation.

2-3 medium baking potatoes
1-2 tbs. full-flavored olive oil
salt and freshly ground pepper

Preheat oven to 400°. Wash potatoes and cut each lengthwise into 8 wedges. Pour oil, salt and pepper into a flat plate. Roll potato wedges to coat with oil. Line a jelly roll pan or cookie sheet that has sides with a sheet of aluminum foil. Stand potato wedges up, with peel side down, on baking sheet. Bake for 25 to 30 minutes until potatoes are puffed and lightly browned. Serve immediately.

GRILLED FLANK STEAK WITH CHIPOTLE CHILE MARINADE

Servings: 2-3

Use canned chipotle chiles in adobo sauce. Serve in warmed burrito-sized tortillas for wrappers, with hot refried beans, tomatoes, shredded lettuce and fresh cilantro.

1¼ lb. flank steak, well trimmed
lime juice

MARINADE
2 tbs. vegetable oil
1 chipotle chile
1 tsp. adobo sauce
grated rind (zest) from 1 orange

¼ cup orange juice
½ tsp. ground cumin
½ tsp. salt
freshly ground pepper

With knife at a 45-degree angle, cut flank steak into ⅛-inch-thin diagonal slices across the grain. Thread steak on metal or presoaked wood skewers, pushing slices close together, forming ribbons. Combine marinade ingredients in a food processor bowl, and process until mixture is quite smooth. Spoon marinade over both sides of steak ribbons and marinade for 20 to 30 minutes. Cook on a preheated grill for 3 to 4 minutes a side, turning once. Squeeze lime juice over cooked steak. Serve immediately.

APPLE-GLAZED PORK STRIPS

This triple-apple-flavored marinade goes together quickly and is a delicious accent for the pork. Look for pretoasted sesame seeds in the Asian food section of your supermarket. They can just be sprinkled on at the last minute.

2 pork tenderloins, about 1 lb. total
2 tbs. apple juice
1 tbs. apple cider vinegar
1 tbs. vegetable oil

3 tbs. apple jelly
1 tbs. Dijon mustard
salt and freshly ground pepper
toasted sesame seeds for garnish

Trim pork tenderloins and cut each tenderloin into strips lengthwise with the grain, about ¼-inch thick. Thread each strip on a metal or presoaked wood skewer and lay flat on a plate or in a glass or stainless steel pan. Combine apple juice, apple cider vinegar and oil. Brush on kabobs and marinate for 30 to 45 minutes in the refrigerator, turning skewers once or twice to distribute marinade. Melt jelly in the microwave for a few seconds, let cool slightly and stir in mustard, salt and pepper. Brush tenderloins with jelly-mustard mixture and cook on a preheated grill over medium heat for about 4 to 5 minutes a side. Brush once or twice during grilling. Sprinkle with sesame seeds and serve.

MARMALADE-GLAZED PORK SKEWERS

Servings: 3-4

*A zesty orange mustard sauce is brushed over the pork strips during grilling. Serve with **Creamy Potato Gratin**, page 127, and a crisp green vegetable. Try this marinade on chicken, too.*

2 pork tenderloins, about 1½ lb. total
1 tbs. lemon juice
1 tbs. vegetable oil

SAUCE

2 tbs. orange marmalade
2 tbs. Dijon mustard
2 tsp. brown sugar

1 tbs. lemon juice
2 tsp. soy sauce

Trim pork tenderloins and cut each lengthwise into 5 strips about ⅜-inch thick. Pound each strip lightly to make flattened slices about ¼-inch thick. Thread each strip on a metal or presoaked wood skewer. Combine lemon juice and vegetable oil; brush over pork strips and allow to stand for 20 to 30 minutes. Place sauce ingredients in a small saucepan. Heat gently to melt marmalade and combine. Remove from heat. Cook pork skewers on a preheated grill over medium heat for about 3 to 4 minutes a side. Brush with sauce 2 or 3 times during grilling. Serve, spooning remaining sauce over meat.

CREAMY POTATO GRATIN

Servings: 3-4

This goes together quickly if you use the food processor to slice the potatoes. Try this with grated Gruyère or Gouda cheese instead of Parmesan, and add a few minced hot peppers or sautéed onion rings between the potato layers.

2 lb. russet potatoes, peeled, thinly
  sliced, about 1/16-inch thick
1 tbs. butter
3 cloves garlic, minced
dash red pepper flakes

salt and freshly ground pepper
1/2 cup grated Parmesan cheese
2/3 cup chicken stock
1/3 cup milk
1/3 cup heavy cream

Spread sliced potatoes on paper towels to remove surface moisture. Preheat oven to 350°. In a 12-inch ovenproof skillet or shallow casserole that is safe for a stove top burner, melt butter. Sauté garlic and red pepper flakes for 1 to 2 minutes to soften garlic. Remove garlic from skillet with a spatula. Place 1/2 of the potato slices in the skillet; sprinkle with sautéed garlic, salt, pepper and 1/2 of the Parmesan cheese. Cover with remaining potatoes. Sprinkle with remaining cheese. Pour in chicken stock, milk and cream. Bring liquid to a boil on top of the stove, and then place in oven. Bake for about 45 minutes, until potatoes are tender and top is lightly browned.

GRILLED ISLAND-STYLE PORK

*Rum and lime juice flavor these succulent grilled pork pieces. Serve with **Black Beans and Rice**, page 129, and slices of fresh sweet pineapple or mango.*

2 pork tenderloins, about 1½ lb. total
2 tbs. dark rum
grated rind (zest) of 1 lime, reserve for sauce
2 tbs. fresh lime juice
1 tbs. vegetable oil
¼ tsp. Tabasco Jalapeño Sauce

½ cup chicken stock
¼ cup brown sugar
1 clove garlic, minced
1 tsp. grated ginger root
salt and freshly ground pepper
1 tsp. cornstarch dissolved in 1 tbs. cold water

Cut each tenderloin in half lengthwise. Pound strips lightly to make them an even thickness. Thread on long skewers, running skewer through center of pork strips. Combine rum, lime juice, vegetable oil and Tabasco; brush on pork strips. Marinate for 20 to 30 minutes. Grill on a preheated grill for about 8 to 10 minutes a side, until pork is no longer pink. Combine remaining marinade, lime zest, chicken stock, sugar, garlic and ginger in a small saucepan. Bring to a boil, reduce heat and simmer for 5 minutes. Season sauce with salt and pepper. Stir in dissolved cornstarch mixture and cook until sauce thickens. Pour sauce through a strainer into a serving bowl. Remove pork from skewers, slice into ¾-inch slices and spoon sauce over meat.

BLACK BEANS AND RICE

This is a variation of a Puerto Rican dish called "Moors and Christians," which cooks in about 25 minutes if you use canned beans. It makes an excellent side dish for grilled meat or chicken.

1 cup chicken stock
½ cup uncooked long-grain rice
salt and freshly ground pepper
2 tbs. vegetable oil
¼ cup chopped onion
¼ cup diced green or red bell pepper
1 small jalapeño, seeded, finely minced
1 clove garlic, minced
1 can (15 oz.) black beans, drained, rinsed with cold water

Bring chicken stock to a boil in a small saucepan; add rice, salt and pepper. Cover and cook over very low heat for about 18 to 20 minutes, until rice is tender. Heat oil in a medium skillet. Sauté onion, peppers and garlic for 8 to 10 minutes until onion is soft, but not browned. Add drained black beans and hot cooked rice. Stir gently to combine. Check seasoning, adding more salt and pepper if needed. Heat mixture for 2 to 3 minutes and pour into a heated serving bowl.

PORK CARNITAS-STYLE

Servings: 6

This is a great party dish and the amounts double easily. The pork can be baked the day before and coated with spices just before grilling. Because the pork is fully cooked, it only needs a few minutes on the grill until it is hot and a nice brown crust has formed. Serve in warm tortillas, top with avocado and tomato pieces, roll up and eat. Serve with **Green Chile and Rice Bake**, *page 103, and a fresh fruit salad.*

3 lb. boneless pork loin, well trimmed,
  cut into 2-inch cubes
1 onion, peeled and sliced
2 cloves garlic, peeled, smashed
2 large carrots, trimmed, sliced
3 cups chicken stock
2 tbs. vegetable oil
3 tbs. prepared chili powder
salt and freshly ground pepper
fresh flour tortillas
Avocado Salsa, follows

Preheat oven to 350°. Place pork cubes in an ovenproof casserole; add onion, garlic, carrots and chicken stock. There should be enough liquid to almost cover meat.

Cover and bake for about 1 hour, or until pork reaches an internal temperature of 165°. Remove from oven, allow pork to cool in liquid and refrigerate.

Remove pork from refrigerator 1 hour before grilling. Discard vegetables and liquid. Pat pork cubes dry with paper towels and toss with vegetable oil. Combine chili powder with salt and pepper, and rub cubes with chili mixture. Allow to marinate for 20 to 30 minutes before grilling. Thread on metal or presoaked wood skewers and grill over a hot fire for 5 to 10 minutes, turning frequently, until pork is hot and outside is brown and crisp.

Warm tortillas in foil. Put meat on a tortilla, add avocado salsa, roll like a burrito and enjoy!

AVOCADO SALSA

3 large ripe avocados, peeled, seeded
3 large ripe fresh tomatoes, peeled, seeded, chopped
1 large jalapeño pepper, finely minced

1 tbs. fresh lime juice
salt and freshly ground pepper
generous amount fresh cilantro leaves

Dice avocados and combine with tomatoes, jalapeño, lime juice, salt and pepper in a serving bowl. Toss to mix well and allow to stand a few minutes so the flavors combine. Toss with cilantro leaves just before serving.

GRILLED SAUSAGES

*Choose two or three favorite kinds of sausages for this recipe. Currant or grape jelly also makes an excellent glaze. Serve with **Lentil Salad**, page 133.*

6 assorted sausages, about 1-inch diameter
red or green bell pepper squares, optional
¼ cup apple jelly, melted

Cut each sausage into 3 chunks. Alternate kinds of sausages with pepper pieces on metal or presoaked wood skewers so each person gets a variety. Grill over medium heat for about 10 minutes, turning frequently, until sausages are nicely browned and juicy. Remove to a serving platter, brush with melted jelly and serve.

LENTIL SALAD

This spicy salad is the perfect accompaniment to grilled sausages or chicken. Any lentil will work in this recipe, but it is particularly good made with tiny green French lentils. This can be done ahead and refrigerated.

1 cup lentils
2½ cups water
2 tbs. sherry vinegar
2 tbs. extra virgin olive oil
1 tsp. Dijon mustard
½ tsp. ground cumin
½ tsp. Tabasco Jalapeño Sauce

salt and freshly ground pepper
4 green onions, white part only, thinly sliced
¼ cup chopped pimiento or roasted red bell pepper pieces
2 tbs. minced fresh parsley

Pick over lentils, wash and place in a saucepan with water. Bring to a boil, lower heat and cook until lentils are tender but not mushy. Green lentils take about 20 to 25 minutes; brown lentils 15 to 20 minutes. Drain well. Pour into a large mixing bowl and while still warm add vinegar, olive oil, mustard, cumin, Tabasco, salt and pepper. Mix well and allow to cool to room temperature. Stir in onions, pimiento and parsley. If done ahead, remove from refrigerator about 30 minutes before serving.

GRILLED LIVER AND BACON
WITH CABERNET ONIONS

Servings: 2

This recipe is for liver lovers and can be expanded to meet the demand.

½ lb. calves' liver, thinly sliced
4-5 slices bacon

oil for brushing
Cabernet Onions, follows

Cut liver pieces lengthwise into 1-inch-wide strips. Precook bacon in a microwave for about 2 minutes or blanch in boiling water for 1 minute. Remove to paper towels to drain. Place half a strip of bacon on each piece of liver and thread a metal or presoaked wood skewer lengthwise through liver and bacon, keeping meat as flat as possible. Brush both sides with oil. Grill on a preheated grill for about 4 to 5 minutes a side, starting with bacon side down. Serve with *Cabernet Onions*.

CABERNET ONIONS

2 medium red onions, thinly sliced
¼ cup Cabernet Sauvignon wine
1 tbs. butter

1 tbs. olive oil
1 tbs. sugar
salt and freshly ground pepper

Combine onions and wine in a medium skillet. Cover and cook for about 15 minutes until onions are soft. Uncover; add butter, oil, sugar, salt and pepper. Increase heat and cook until wine has evaporated.

SKEWERED HAM AND DRIED APRICOTS

Here is a great way to serve the rest of the holiday ham.

12-14 ham pieces, cut into 1½- or 2-inch squares
12-14 dried apricots, softened in boiling water and well drained
1 tbs. soy sauce
1 tbs. honey
½ tsp. grated ginger root
1 tbs. vegetable oil
toasted sesame seeds for garnish, optional

Arrange ham pieces and apricots on metal or presoaked wood skewers, alternating meat and fruit. Combine remaining ingredients, except sesame seeds, and brush over ham and apricots. Cook on a preheated grill over medium heat for 4 to 6 minutes until ham is hot and apricot edges are lightly browned. Sprinkle with toasted sesame seeds if desired.

HOISIN-GLAZED HAM
AND PINEAPPLE KABOBS

Servings: 2-3

This is made with a delicious, quick glaze. When in season, substitute pieces of fresh peach, plum or apricot for the pineapple. In winter when fresh fruit is in limited supply, use dried apricots or prunes that have been softened in boiling water. Check the ethnic section of your supermarket for hoisin sauce and toasted sesame seeds.

12-14 ham pieces, cut into 1½- or 2-inch squares
12-14 fresh pineapple pieces, about same size as ham pieces
2 tbs. hoisin sauce
2 tsp. vegetable oil
toasted sesame seeds, optional

Alternate ham and pineapple pieces on metal or presoaked wood skewers. Combine hoisin sauce with vegetable oil and brush over ham and pineapple pieces. Cook on a preheated grill over medium heat for 4 to 6 minutes, turning once or twice, until ham and pineapple are hot. Sprinkle with toasted sesame seeds if desired.

HAM KABOBS WITH MANDARIN ORANGE SAUCE

This sauce is also terrific with pork tenderloin kabobs, chicken chunks and many other grilled entrées. Steamed rice and sugar snap peas make a pretty combination.

12-14 ham pieces, cut into 1½- or 2-inch
  squares
1-2 tsp. vegetable oil
1 can (15 oz.) Mandarin orange segments
  in light syrup

2 tbs. Triple Sec or orange liqueur
1 tbs. lemon juice
1 tbs. Dijon mustard
2 tbs. cornstarch dissolved in 2 tbs.
  orange liquid

Arrange ham pieces on metal or presoaked wood skewers. Brush with vegetable oil. Drain juice from oranges, reserving liquid. Set aside 2 tbs. orange liquid to dissolve cornstarch. Pour remaining liquid in a blender container or food processor bowl. Reserve 8 to 10 orange segments and add remaining orange pieces to blender. Add Triple Sec, lemon juice and mustard to blender. Process until well combined but not completely smooth. Pour mixture into a small saucepan and bring to a boil, reduce heat and simmer for 5 minutes. Dissolve cornstarch in reserved orange liquid and add to hot sauce. Stir until sauce thickens. Cook ham pieces on a preheated grill over medium heat for 4 to 5 minutes until hot and lightly browned. Serve with hot sauce.

SKEWERED BLUE CHEESE MEATBALLS

Servings: 2-3

Tiny pieces of blue cheese melt inside the meatballs during grilling. Serve with ketchup, cole slaw and lots of French bread.

1 lb. ground sirloin or lean ground turkey
1 egg white
1/4 tsp. salt
generous amount freshly ground pepper
1/4 tsp. garlic powder
2 tbs. red wine
1 tsp. Dijon mustard
1/4 cup crushed cracker crumbs
1/2 cup (2 oz.) crumbled blue cheese

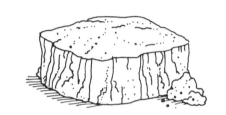

Combine ingredients, except blue cheese, and mix well, using hands. Gently distribute cheese throughout mixture. Form into 1-inch balls and arrange 3 or 4 meatballs on each presoaked bamboo skewer. Place formed skewers on a tray, cover and refrigerate for at least 1 hour to firm meat.

Oil grill rack and grill over hot coals for about 12 to 14 minutes, turning frequently. Meatballs will be very tender, so use a spatula to help turn them over. Serve immediately.

GRILLED VEGETABLE SKEWERS

Grilled vegetables are tantalizing to watch and smell while grilling and even more wonderful to eat. Summer's bounty of eggplant, squash and tiny potatoes grill beautifully. Always grill more vegetables than you need for one meal and use them to put together a quick pasta, grilled vegetable risotto or pizza topping.

Grilling is the perfect way to roast and peel peppers, as well. The onion family is a natural for grilling, and grilled onions taste as delicious as they smell while cooking. Baby leeks grilled and served with a simple orange sauce make an elegant accompaniment for fish or chicken. Try grilling cremini, huge Portobello, shiitake or supermarket white button mushrooms to accompany grilled meats or fish.

Asparagus, carrots and even cauliflower can be grilled and served with a special sauce or a light dribble of good olive oil. We precook the firmer vegetables in the microwave for a minute or two to shorten the cooking time on the grill. A special treat is to roll almost cooked small new Yukon Gold or yellow Finnish potatoes in olive oil seasoned with fresh herbs and then finish cooking them on the grill. They have a very creamy texture and unique taste.

We like to serve grilled vegetables as a first course, or use a combination of grilled dishes with some fresh foccacia or cornbread for a perfect summer lunch. *Grilled Baby Leeks with Orange Sauce* and *Grilled Asparagus with Tofu Sesame Sauce* are great starters. Many grilled vegetables can be served as party finger food, using the sauce as a dip.

Simple grilled vegetables can be presented Italian-style with a drizzle of good olive oil to add to the flavor and moistness.

Vegetables generally should be cooked over a medium hot fire or grill to give them time to soften and to allow their natural sugars to caramelize. Arrange vegetables requiring similar cooking times on the same skewer, or the little green onions will be done long before the carrots.

A quick tip — nonstick vegetable cooking spray works just as well as brushing with oil, and when you spray there is no brush to wash.

Grilled vegetables are delicious! Try them and see.

ABOUT GRILLING ASPARAGUS

- Using skewers to grill asparagus makes it easy to turn several spears at the same time. Run 2 skewers placed about 1 inch apart through middle of the spears.

- Medium or large fat asparagus spears work better for grilling because they have a large enough diameter to pierce with skewers.

- It is not necessary to peel asparagus spears, but do wash them well.

- Asparagus will cook faster if blanched in hot boiling water for 1 to 2 minutes before threading on the skewers.

- If you don't precook asparagus, soak it in cold water for 15 to 20 minutes as the Italians do, and allow about 12 to 15 minutes grilling time for smaller spears over a fairly low fire.

- Asparagus should be cooked until it can easily be pierced with tip of a knife.

- Asparagus brushed with full-flavored olive oil before grilling makes terrific finger food for a party.

GRILLED ASPARAGUS WITH
TOFU SESAME SAUCE

Serve this as a first course on colorful plates, garnished with tiny black olives and orange slices, or as a side dish for grilled fish. It is nice paired with other grilled vegetable dishes, and can be served hot or at room temperature.

1 lb. fresh asparagus, washed, trimmed
olive oil for brushing

TOFU SESAME SAUCE

1/4 cup soft tofu
2 tbs. chicken stock
1 tbs. sesame oil
1 tbs. vegetable or peanut oil

2 tbs. rice wine vinegar
1 tbs. minced ginger root
salt and white pepper

Blanch asparagus in boiling salted water for 2 minutes. Remove, rinse with cold water and drain well on paper towels. Brush spears with olive oil and arrange on skewers. Grill over medium heat for 10 to 12 minutes until lightly browned and tender. Combine remaining ingredients in a blender container and process until smooth. Arrange grilled asparagus on a serving platter or individual plates and pour sauce over spears.

GRILLED ASPARAGUS WITH ROASTED GARLIC MAYONNAISE

Asparagus and mayonnaise are a classic combination. This mayonnaise-based sauce is flavored with creamy roasted garlic and lightened with a little sour cream. Try this sauce with grilled artichokes, too. For roasting garlic, see page 115.

ROASTED GARLIC MAYONNAISE

1/2 cup mayonnaise
4 cloves roasted garlic, mashed into a
  fairly smooth paste
grated rind (zest) from 1 lemon

1 tbs. fresh lemon juice
2 tbs. light sour cream
dash Tabasco Jalapeño Sauce
salt and white pepper

1 lb. asparagus, washed, trimmed
olive oil for brushing

Combine mayonnaise with remaining sauce ingredients in a small bowl and mix well. Refrigerate until ready to serve. Blanch asparagus in boiling, salted water for 2 minutes, drain and rinse with cold water. Pat dry on paper towels. Place asparagus on skewers, brush with olive oil and grill over medium heat until tender. Serve dipping sauce in individual small bowls, or pass a larger bowl.

GRILLED ASPARAGUS
WITH LEMON SESAME GLAZE

This is a great side dish for grilled fish or chicken dishes.

1 lb. asparagus, washed, trimmed
vegetable oil for brushing

LEMON SESAME GLAZE
⅓ cup chicken stock
1 tbs. honey
grated rind (zest) from 1 lemon

1 tsp. cornstarch
2 tbs. fresh lemon juice
½ tsp. sesame oil

Blanch asparagus in boiling salted water for 2 minutes. Drain, rinse with cold water and pat dry with paper towels. Thread asparagus on metal or presoaked wood skewers and brush with vegetable oil. Grill over medium heat for 10 to 12 minutes until asparagus is lightly browned and tender.

Combine chicken stock, honey and lemon zest in a small saucepan. Bring mixture to a boil. Dissolve cornstarch in 2 tbs. lemon juice, add to chicken stock and cook until mixture thickens. Stir in sesame oil. Spoon glaze over grilled asparagus, or use as a dipping sauce.

ABOUT GRILLING CARROTS

Grilling brings out the wonderful caramel flavor of carrots.

- Brush or spray with a little olive or vegetable oil before grilling.
- It is easier to grill carrots if they are lightly precooked before grilling. Peel and cut carrots into pieces of similar lengths. Place in a microwavable dish with 2 to 3 tbs. water, cover and cook for 2 to 3 minutes on high, or until carrots can be pierced with a fork, but are not soft. Check after 2 minutes and remove smaller pieces as they become done. Remove from dish and drain on paper towels.
- Alternately, blanch carrot pieces in boiling water for about 5 minutes, or until they can be pierced with a knife tip. Drain and dry on paper towels.
- Carrot pieces with similar diameters should be arranged together on skewers for better control over grilling time.
- Use two skewers placed about 1 inch apart through center of carrots to keep carrots from rolling while turning. A larger, flat-bladed skewer works well, too.
- If grilling carrots without skewers, cut unblanched carrots into $1/4$-inch-thick slices, brush with oil, and grill on a barbecue screen or mesh to prevent carrots from falling through the grill rack.

LIME AND CURRY GRILLED CARROTS

Servings: 3-4

Curry powder complements the natural sweetness of carrots.

1 lb. carrots, trimmed, peeled
2-3 tbs. water
2 tbs. vegetable oil
1 tsp. curry powder
grated rind (zest) from 1 lime
1 tbs. fresh lime juice
salt and freshly ground pepper

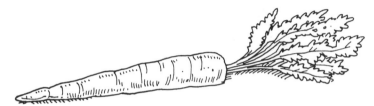

Cut carrots into 1½- or 2-inch chunks. Microwave carrots with 2 to 3 tbs. water in a microwavable dish, covered, for about 4 minutes. Remove from bowl and pat dry with paper towels. Pour vegetable oil into a small skillet; add curry powder and lime zest. Heat gently for 1 to 2 minutes to release curry flavor. Remove from heat and stir in lime juice, salt and pepper. Arrange carrot chunks on metal or presoaked wood skewers. Brush with curry mixture. Grill over medium heat for about 8 to 10 minutes, turning 3 or 4 times, and brushing again with curry oil.

GRILLED CARROTS WITH BLOOD ORANGE SAUCE

This pretty red sauce will cook while the carrots are grilling. Use a lemon zester to make long strips of orange rind. Regular oranges can be used when blood oranges aren't in season. Try this sauce on grilled pork kabobs, too.

1 lb. carrots, peeled, trimmed, blanched
vegetable oil for brushing

Cut carrots into 1½- to 2-inch pieces and arrange carrots on metal or presoaked wood skewers. Brush with oil and cook on a preheated grill for about 10 to 12 minutes, or until lightly browned and tender. Serve sauce over grilled carrots.

BLOOD ORANGE SAUCE

strips of rind (zest) from 1 blood orange
½ cup blood orange juice from 2
  medium oranges
½ tsp. grated ginger root

1 tbs. sugar
1 tbs. butter
2 tsp. cornstarch dissolved in 1 tbs.
  lemon juice

Combine zest, orange juice, ginger, sugar and butter in a small saucepan; bring to a boil. Dissolve cornstarch in lemon juice and add to saucepan. Cook for 3 to 4 minutes until sauce thickens.

GRILLED CURRIED CAULIFLOWER

Cauliflower is given an East Indian accent with a light curry sauce.

1 lb. cauliflower florets
2 tbs. butter
1 tsp. curry powder
½ cup apple juice

Cut the cauliflower florets into similar-sized pieces, about 1½ inches. Place in a microwavable dish with 2 to 3 tbs. water, cover and microwave for 4 minutes, or until crisp-tender. Remove cover and allow to cool enough to handle. Arrange florets on metal or presoaked wood skewers. Melt butter in a small saucepan, add curry powder and cook over low heat for 1 to 2 minutes. Add apple juice, bring to a boil and simmer for 5 minutes.

Brush cauliflower with marinade and grill over medium heat for 3 to 4 minutes a side, or until lightly browned and completely cooked. Brush with marinade once or twice while grilling. Bring remaining marinade to a boil over high heat and cook for 2 to 3 minutes to reduce slightly. Pour over grilled cauliflower and serve.

GRILLED EGGPLANT KABOBS
WITH TAHINI SAUCE

Grilled smoky eggplant chunks are topped with a wonderful garlicky sesame sauce. This sauce also makes a great dip for grilled hot new potatoes, or crisp carrot and celery sticks. Tahini sesame sauce is available in Middle Eastern food shops.

4-5 Japanese eggplants
1/4 cup olive oil

2 tbs. lemon juice

Trim and peel eggplant. Cut into 3/4-inch slices, cutting larger slices in half. Toss with olive oil and lemon juice. Thread on metal or presoaked wood skewers and grill over medium heat for 10 to 12 minutes, turning frequently, until eggplant is cooked and nicely browned. Serve with *Tahini Sauce*.

TAHINI SAUCE

1/4 cup tahini sesame sauce, or 2 tbs.
  smooth peanut butter
2 tbs. water
2 tbs. lemon juice

1 clove garlic, finely minced
1/4 tsp. salt
fresh parsley or cilantro leaves for garnish

Combine all sauce ingredients, except parsley or cilantro, and stir until smooth. If sauce is too thick to spoon easily, stir in a little more water.

GRILLED BABY LEEKS
WITH ORANGE SAUCE

Choose small leeks about the diameter of a nickel, or even a dime, for grilling.

12 baby leeks
olive oil

To prepare leeks, cut off green tops and use only white part of leek. Trim root end and remove one layer of leek leaves. Carefully split leeks vertically very close to the root end, and keep them together as much as possible. Gently run cold water between each leaf to wash out any sand. Push leek halves together and push a metal or presoaked wood skewer through the horizontal center. Arrange remaining leeks on skewer in the same manner. Brush well with olive oil. Grill over medium heat for about 5 to 7 minutes a side, or until tender. Turn once or twice while grilling. Remove from skewer and top with *Orange Sauce*.

ORANGE SAUCE
rind (zest) from 1 orange
⅓ cup fresh orange juice

1 tbs. butter

Use a lemon zester to make long slender strips of orange zest. Combine orange zest, juice and butter in a small saucepan. Bring to a boil and cook over medium heat for 2 to 3 minutes to soften zest and slightly reduce sauce.

GRILLED LEEKS WITH ROMESCO DIP

Servings: 4

*Grilled leeks are terrific with a Spanish **Romesco Dip** of roasted red peppers, almonds, garlic and onion.*

8-10 small leeks, about ¾-inch diameter
olive oil for brushing
1 cup *Romesco Dip*, page 21

To prepare leeks, cut off green tops and use only white part of leek. Trim root end and remove one layer of leek leaves. Carefully split leeks vertically very close to the root end, and keep them together as much as possible. Gently run cold water between each leaf to wash out any sand. Push two leek halves together and push a metal or presoaked wood skewer through the horizontal center. Arrange remaining leeks on skewer in the same manner. Brush well with olive oil. Grill over medium heat for about 10 minutes per side, or until tender. Turn once or twice while grilling. Remove from skewer and serve with *Romesco Dip*.

GRILLED ONION WEDGES

Servings: 2

Onions can be cut and skewered ahead of time and kept covered until you are ready to cook them. The illustration shows you how to place the onions on a skewer. Increase the recipe to meet the demand.

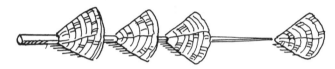

1 medium yellow, white or red onion
olive oil for brushing

Peel and trim onion. Remove outer layer of skin. Cut onion in half from stem to root; cut each half into 3 equal wedges. Push a metal or presoaked wood skewer through middle of onion wedge, starting at the top of the onion triangle. This will hold all onion leaves together during grilling. Place all onion wedges on the same skewer or divide on 2 skewers. Brush with olive oil and grill over medium heat for about 15 minutes, turning once or twice during grilling. Onions should be brown, crispy and tender.

NOTE: Onions can be cut into ½-thick slices, with the outside layers of skin intact, and then threaded through the center of the slice on a wide, flat skewer.

BASIC GRILLED MUSHROOMS

Grilled fresh mushrooms are not to be missed. They just need a light brushing of oil and take on a slightly smoky flavor when grilled. There is an ever-increasing variety of fresh mushrooms on the market today. A real treat is grilled large Portobello mushrooms that average about 5 to 6 inches across, because they have a very meaty and substantial taste. The cremini mushroom is about the same size as the white cultivated mushrooms commonly available, and it has a more pronounced mushroom flavor. Fresh shiitake mushrooms also grill well — just pull out the tough stem, brush with oil and grill.

Grilled mushrooms are a marvelous accompaniment to grilled meats or chicken, or can be served as part of a grilled vegetable platter. Use your favorite kinds of mushrooms. Tuck in small green onion pieces between the mushrooms, if you like.

12-16 medium-sized fresh mushrooms — white button, cremini or shiitake
garlic-flavored or plain olive oil

Clean mushrooms and cut off stem at base of cap. Arrange on metal or presoaked wood skewers, pushing skewer through center of each mushroom. Brush with olive oil and grill over medium heat for 4 to 5 minutes a side.

GRILLED NEW POTATOES

New potatoes, particularly the Yukon Gold and Finnish varieties, are wonderful when grilled. Precook the potatoes and grill at the last minute.

12-16 small new potatoes, about 1½-2 inch diameter
1 tbs. full-flavored olive oil
salt and freshly ground pepper

Place potatoes in a large saucepan, cover with cold water, place a lid on the pan and cook for about 20 to 25 minutes, or until barely tender. Drain and allow to stand until you are ready to grill. Or cook in microwave. Pour olive oil on a flat plate, season with salt and pepper, and roll cooked potatoes in oil until all sides are coated. Arrange potatoes on metal or presoaked wood skewers, and cook on a preheated grill for about 10 to 15 minutes, turning once or twice until all sides are nicely browned. Serve immediately.

VARIATION

Add ground cumin, a pinch of cayenne pepper or fresh herbs to the olive oil to coat the potatoes.

GRILLED SWEET POTATOES AND KUMQUATS

Sweet potatoes or yams are delicious with only a light brush of oil before grilling. The kumquats soften and add a nice citrus-flavored accent. Try softened dried apricots or chunks of fresh mango, too.

1 large sweet potato or yam, about 10 oz.
1/4 cup water
10-12 ripe kumquats
vegetable oil for brushing

Peel sweet potato and cut into 1-inch chunks. Place sweet potato chunks in a microwavable dish with water. Cover and cook on HIGH for about 3 to 4 minutes, or until potato chunks are almost cooked through and can be pierced with a knife tip. Drain and allow to cool enough to handle. Alternate potato chunks with kumquats on metal or presoaked wood skewers. Brush lightly with vegetable oil and cook on a preheated grill for about 6 to 8 minutes a side, or until potatoes are lightly browned.

GRILLED VEGETABLES
WITH MOROCCAN SAUCE

This spicy garlic sauce is terrific on grilled vegetables, grilled fish or chicken.

MOROCCAN SAUCE

1 clove garlic
1/4 cup loosely packed fresh parsley
  leaves
1/4 cup loosely packed fresh cilantro
  leaves
5-6 fresh mint leaves

1/4 cup full-flavored olive oil
2 tbs. lemon juice
1 tsp. ground cumin
1/2 tsp. paprika
1/2 tsp. Tabasco Jalapeño Sauce
salt and freshly ground pepper

vegetable assortment of choice: zucchini, summer squash, mushrooms, eggplant,
  blanched carrots, cooked new potatoes or sweet potato chunks, etc.

Using a food processor, process garlic, parsley, cilantro and mint leaves until finely
chopped. Add remaining sauce ingredients and process until blended.
  Prepare vegetables, arrange on skewers, brush with sauce and grill over medium
heat until vegetables are nicely browned and tender when pierced with a knife tip. Pass
remaining sauce to spoon over vegetables.

LEMON-HERBED VEGETABLES

*Choose your favorite vegetables — the more colorful, the better — for these skewers. If you have time, grill a second batch of vegetables when you have a nice fire, and use them for **Grilled Vegetable Risotto**, page 162, or **Pasta Primavera**, page 166.*

3-4 red, green and yellow bell peppers
4 zucchini
3 small Japanese eggplants
4 yellow summer squash
8 cherry tomatoes
8-10 medium mushrooms
1 small red onion

BASTING SAUCE
$1/4$ cup olive oil
2 tbs. lemon juice
2 tbs. vermouth or white wine
$1/2$ tsp. sugar
2 tsp. Italian herb seasoning
salt and freshly ground pepper

Cut peppers into quarters, or sixths if they are large. Remove stem and seeds. Trim zucchini, eggplants and summer squash. Cut into 1-inch chunks. Remove stems from mushroom caps. Trim onion ends and cut into 8 wedges. Push skewer through middle of onion wedge, starting at top of wedge. Arrange vegetables with similar cooking times together on skewers (grilling times follow).

Combine olive oil with remaining *Basting Sauce* ingredients, mixing well. Brush vegetable skewers generously with herb mixture and allow to stand at room temperature for 15 to 20 minutes. Brush again and cook on a preheated grill over medium heat, turning several times, until vegetables are nicely browned and tender.

GRILLING TIMES

cherry tomatoes	4 to 5 minutes
squash	4 to 5 minutes
eggplant	4 to 5 minutes
peppers	5 to 6 minutes
mushrooms	6 to 8 minutes
onions	10 to 12 minutes

AROMATIC BUTTER SAUCES
FOR GRILLED VEGETABLES

Compound butters can be made ahead and refrigerated or frozen. Serve thin slices to melt over hot vegetables as they come off the grill, or heat for a sauce.

For each recipe: Combine ingredients in a small bowl, mixing well. Form into a small log, about 1 inch diameter, on a sheet of waxed paper or kitchen foil. Roll in paper and refrigerate for 1 to 2 hours to harden. Cut into 1/4-inch slices to serve.

GREEN HERBED BUTTER

Try this with grilled potatoes, squash or carrots.

3 tbs. butter, softened
1 tsp. minced shallot
2 tbs. finely chopped fresh parsley

1 tbs. finely chopped fresh basil leaves
pinch red pepper flakes
salt and freshly ground pepper

ORANGE GINGER BUTTER

This is delicious with grilled carrots, asparagus, sweet potatoes and fennel.

3 tbs. butter, softened
1 green onion, white part only, finely
  chopped

grated rind (zest) from 1 orange
1 tsp. grated ginger root
salt and freshly ground pepper

LEMON MINT BUTTER

Use this on your favorite grilled vegetables or fish.

3 tbs. butter, softened
grated rind (zest) from 1 lemon
1/4 tsp. lemon extract

6-8 small fresh mint leaves, finely
  chopped
salt and freshly ground pepper

SUN-DRIED TOMATO BUTTER

Small new potatoes, carrots and eggplant are great with this butter.

3 tbs. butter, softened
1/2 tsp. ground cumin
2-3 drops Tabasco Jalapeño Sauce

3-4 small oil-packed sun-dried
  tomatoes, finely chopped
1 green onion, white part only, finely
  chopped

TARRAGON BUTTER

This is a terrific accent for grilled carrots, potatoes or squash.

3 tbs. butter, softened
1 tsp. tarragon vinegar or white wine
  vinegar

2 tbs. chopped fresh tarragon leaves
salt and freshly ground pepper

GRILLED VEGETABLE RISOTTO

Use Italian arborio rice, or substitute a medium-grain California rice such as Silver Pearl. This delicious one-dish meal takes about 20 minutes of last-minute stirring, but you can grill the vegetables a day ahead and cut them up just before adding to the rice. Serve with some crusty garlic bread and a crisp Verdicchio or Sauvignon Blanc wine.

3-4 cups chicken stock
1 tbs. olive oil
1 tbs. butter
½ cup finely chopped onion
1 clove garlic, minced
dash red pepper flakes
1 cup uncooked short-grain rice
1½ cups diced (½-inch) grilled vegetables
salt and freshly ground pepper
2 medium tomatoes, peeled, seeded, diced
⅓ cup grated Parmesan cheese
2 tbs. finely chopped fresh parsley
grated Parmesan cheese

Heat chicken stock to simmering in a small saucepan. In a heavy saucepan, heat olive oil and butter, add onion and sauté for 5 to 6 minutes until soft. Add garlic and red pepper flakes and cook another minute. Add rice and stir over low heat for 1 to 2 minutes, coating rice with oil. Using a ladle or measuring cup, add about ½ cup hot chicken stock to rice, stirring until liquid is absorbed. Continue to add ⅓ to ½ cup liquid at a time, always stirring until stock is absorbed. Cook until rice is almost tender but still has a little resistance to the bite. Stir in diced vegetables, salt, pepper and tomatoes. Raise heat and cook for 3 to 4 minutes until mixture is hot. Stir in ⅓ cup Parmesan cheese. Pour into a warm serving bowl, sprinkle with parsley and pass additional Parmesan cheese.

PIZZA WITH GRILLED VEGETABLES

Servings: 4

Leftover grilled vegetables make a wonderful pizza topping. Our favorites are grilled red peppers, sweet onions and mushrooms, but you may prefer others. This is a quick crust recipe that can be done in about 30 minutes.

QUICK PIZZA CRUST

1½ tbs. rapid rising yeast
1½ tsp. light brown sugar
½ cup warm water
3 cups flour

¾ tsp. salt
½ cup warm water
2 tbs. olive oil

TOPPING

1 tsp. full-flavored olive oil
1½ cups grated mozzarella cheese
2 cups coarsely chopped grilled
  vegetable pieces
salt and freshly ground pepper

dash red pepper flakes
½ cup grated Parmesan cheese
2 small fresh tomatoes, peeled, seeded,
  chopped for garnish
fresh basil, thyme or parsley for garnish

Preheat oven to 450°. Dissolve yeast and brown sugar in ½ cup warm water in a small bowl. Let stand 5 minutes until bubbles form. Place flour and salt in food processor bowl and pulse to combine. With food processor running, add yeast mixture, water and olive oil through pouring tube. Process for 2 to 3 minutes until dough forms a ball and comes away from sides of bowl. Remove dough from processor and flatten slightly. Place on an oiled 11-x-15-inch jelly-roll pan and allow to rest for 10 minutes. Gently press dough evenly to fill pan.

Brush pizza crust with olive oil. Sprinkle grated mozzarella cheese evenly over crust. Top with vegetables, salt and pepper, a few red pepper flakes and Parmesan cheese. Bake until crust is lightly browned and cheese is melted, about 15 to 20 minutes. Sprinkle baked pizza with chopped fresh tomatoes and fresh herbs. Cut into wedges and serve.

PASTA PRIMAVERA

Here is another quick and delicious entrée if you have some leftover grilled **Lemon-Herbed Vegetables**, *page 158.*

8 oz. dried pasta shapes, bow ties, spirals or orecchiette
2 tbs. full-flavored olive oil
½ cup chopped onion, optional
8-10 medium mushrooms, sliced, optional
2½-3 cups grilled vegetables, cut into ¾-inch chunks
½ cup chicken stock

2 tbs. heavy cream
dash red pepper flakes
salt and freshly ground pepper
⅓ cup slivered oil-packed sun-dried tomatoes
10-12 fresh basil leaves, cut into thin strips
grated Parmesan cheese

Cook pasta according to package directions. While pasta is cooking, heat oil in a large skillet. Sauté onions and mushrooms, if using, for 3-4 minutes. Add grilled vegetable pieces and toss with oil. Add chicken stock, bring to boil, reduce heat and add heavy cream, red pepper flakes, salt, pepper and sun-dried tomatoes. When pasta is cooked, drain, and pour pasta into skillet with vegetables. Toss over heat for 1 to 2 minutes. Pour pasta into a warmed serving bowl, garnish with basil leaves and serve immediately. Pass Parmesan cheese.

INDEX

SERVE CREATIVE, EASY, NUTRITIOUS MEALS WITH NITTY GRITTY® COOKBOOKS

The Best Bagels Are Made at Home
The Toaster Oven Cookbook
Skewer Cooking on the Grill
Creative Mexican Cooking
Extra-Special Crockery Pot Recipes
Cooking in Clay
Marinades
Deep Fried Indulgences
Cooking with Parchment Paper
The Garlic Cookbook
Flatbreads From Around the World
From Your Ice Cream Maker
Favorite Cookie Recipes
Cappuccino/Espresso: The Book of
   Beverages
Indoor Grilling
Slow Cooking
The Best Pizza Is Made at Home
The Well Dressed Potato
Convection Oven Cookery

The Steamer Cookbook
The Pasta Machine Cookbook
The Versatile Rice Cooker
The Dehydrator Cookbook
The Bread Machine Cookbook
The Bread Machine Cookbook II
The Bread Machine Cookbook III
The Bread Machine Cookbook IV
The Bread Machine Cookbook V
The Bread Machine Cookbook VI
Worldwide Sourdoughs From Your
   Bread Machine
Recipes for the Pressure Cooker
The New Blender Book
The Sandwich Maker Cookbook
Waffles
The Coffee Book
The Juicer Book
The Juicer Book II
Bread Baking (traditional), revised

No Salt, No Sugar, No Fat
   Cookbook
Cooking for 1 or 2
Quick and Easy Pasta Recipes
The 9x13 Pan Cookbook
Chocolate Cherry Tortes and
   Other Lowfat Delights
Low Fat American Favorites
Now That's Italian!
Fabulous Fiber Cookery
Low Salt, Low Sugar, Low Fat
   Desserts
Healthy Cooking on the Run
Healthy Snacks for Kids
Muffins, Nut Breads and More
The Wok
New Ways to Enjoy Chicken
Favorite Seafood Recipes
New International Fondue Cookbook

Write or call for our free catalog.
BRISTOL PUBLISHING ENTERPRISES, INC.
P.O. Box 1737, San Leandro, CA 94577
(800) 346-4889; in California (510) 895-4461